The
MANIFESTO
Project

Akron Series in Contemporary Poetics
Mary Biddinger and John Gallaher, Editors
Jay Robinson and Nick Sturm, Associate Editors

Mary Biddinger, John Gallaher, eds., *The Monkey & the Wrench: Essays into Contemporary Poetics*
Robert Archambeau, *The Poet Resigns: Poetry in a Difficult World*
Rebecca Hazelton & Alan Michael Parker, eds., *The Manifesto Project*

The
MANIFESTO
Project

Edited by
Rebecca Hazelton &
Alan Michael Parker

The University of Akron Press
Akron, Ohio

New Material Copyright © 2017 by The University of Akron Press

All rights reserved · First Edition 2017 · Manufactured in the United States of America. · All inquiries and permission requests should be addressed to the Publisher, the University of Akron Press, Akron, Ohio 44325-1703.

21   20   19   18   17   5   4   3   2   1

ISBN: 978-1-629220-49-9 (paper)
ISBN: 978-1-629220-50-5 (ePDF)
ISBN: 978-1-629220-51-2 (ePub)

A catalog record for this title is available from the Library of Congress.

The paper used in this publication meets the minimum requirements of ANSI NISO Z 39.48–1992 (Permanence of Paper). ∞

Cover: Felicia van Bork, *How to Breathe Again*, 2016, monotype collage, 30 x 22 in. Photo: Christopher Clamp, Jerald Melberg Gallery, www.jeraldmelberg.com. Reproduced with permission. Cover design by Tyler Krusinski.

The Manifesto Project was designed and typeset by Amy Freels. The typeface, Mrs. Eaves, was designed by Zuzana Licko in 1996. The display type, Oswald, was designed by Vernon Adams in 2012. *The Manifesto Project* was printed on sixty-pound natural and bound by Bookmasters of Ashland, Ohio.

Contents

Introduction
More Manifestos, Please

When we announced the call for submissions for *The Manifesto Project*, many poets and writers shared the link to the project on social media, expressing support and interest in reading the book. They were specific in their support, not just sharing and "liking," but saying, "this is needed" and "I have always wanted something like this." Some even contacted us regarding use of the text in the classroom. One woman seemed to want us to use her lesson plan as a manifesto.

But despite such enthusiasm for sharing the open call and for the project itself, many early enthusiasts did not themselves submit. Younger poets begged off, telling us they weren't established enough. Older poets were too busy. Although we ultimately had a great response and had to choose between great options, it was clear that had this book merely been a poetry anthology, we would have been flooded with submissions from the get-go. It was the writing of a manifesto that gave people pause.

Why is that? One thousand words of prose is nothing, even for a poet, and the call was very broad and open to interpretation. We didn't put clear parameters on what we thought a manifesto was; not that we knew what a contemporary manifesto would look like. Our own initial conceptions of a manifesto mainly came from early twentieth century examples, such as the Futurists and Dada, or a little later, pretty much anything Pound wrote about his feelings, or a standard, Frank O'Hara's "Personism," which parodies the idea of a manifesto and then somehow turns achingly sincere.

None of these, however, seems exactly relevant today, and there's a reason for that. Manifestos are responses to their current circumstances:

political, economic, technological (and more). Manifestos assess the current situation, and look to the future. They aren't just descriptive, they're prescriptive—they are calls for action and demands for change, either implicitly or explicitly. Manifestos are inherently revolutionary, and because of this, they have an expiration date—the status quo and the revolutions it inspires ever-shifting. We just don't know when that date will be. It's only later that we look at something like The Declaration of Independence and say, "Okay, that's great, way to found the country, but why "all men" and not "all people?" Why is it that you really meant "all *white* men and no ladies"? Also, that Creator mention is just going to be a headache later. Donna Harraway's "Cyborg Manifesto" was the newest and greatest in the mid '90s, but now seems pretty self-evident. The egalitarian claims put forth in "The Hacker's Manifesto" are a little harder to swallow in light of the recent #gamergate on twitter, the doxxing of female game designers, and the harassment of Anita Sarkesian. None of this is necessarily due to a lack of vision on the writer's part—the circumstances have changed. For a manifesto to remain relevant, it would also have to be fungible, and adaptable to circumstances.

The manifestos in this volume reflect our contemporary circumstances. They zing with zeitgeist. Some, like "The Racial Imaginary" by Beth Loffreda and Claudia Rankine, or Orlando Menes's "Manifesto," concern the intersections of racial or cultural identity and writing. Others confront gender (among other things), such as Valerie Wetlaufer's "Inscribing the Domestic Daily," or Stephen Burt's "Manifest Stephanie." There are global perspectives here, such as Susan Briante's "Big Data Birdsong," which examines the place of poetry in a world of big data, or Kara Candito's "Destroy Yourself!: Some Notes on the Poetics of Travel." Several manifestos look at poetic composition, and many manifestos are concerned with what poetry can *do* and what it *doesn't* do. There are *-isms* here, as in Jacqueline Osherow's "Opportunism" and Joshua Robbins and Jeffrey Schultz's "Subscendentalism." There are manifestos that draw from a long lineage of prior manifestos, and there's more than one manifesto that denies the very notion of a manifesto. The poets in this anthology differ widely, which makes their points of commonality all the more startling.

In assembling this anthology, we asked each poet to give us two poems along with his or her manifesto. As typical anthology practice goes, this might seem a bit backward. The usual order of operations is that a poet writes a poem, someone deems it to be Good, and the poem is henceforth enshrined in an anthology. For this project, however, we thought to hand the sacred oils over to the authors themselves, so that they could anoint as they saw fit. The poets are, after all, the ones declaring the principles. Let's see those principles in action.

The world of poetry can seem very small in comparison to other arts, such as music and film, which have cultural and monetary cachet, and miniscule in the general world of commerce. Poets easily feel isolated and ineffectual. But poets have opinions galore, and think of their work in so many different ways—and are willing, as we see in this volume, to step on toes.

Stepping on toes has value. Calling for change, even a small change, can have wider repercussions, can cast doubt on larger institutions. It's revolutionary. Whether you agree with him or not, when Donald Hall criticized the "McPoem" for its bland, safe, generic qualities, the logical extension of that critique was a criticism of the MFA system that spawned such results. What are the artistic repercussions of an educational system—an expensive one at that—aimed at "producing" artists? We don't have answers to this challenging question; we're both products of this system, and nonetheless poets who aim to maintain our skepticism regarding its legacy.

It can seem ludicrous to suggest that poetry can speak truth to power, but poems have undone governments, not just feelings about governments. We can feel hopeless and do nothing, or we can do whatever we want. It is our hope that any poets, or future poets, reading this book will find something they love in here, as well as something with which they violently disagree. We hope you read a poem, read the poet's manifesto, then read the poet's second poem. Read three manifestos in a row, at random, then the authors' poems. Read poem upon poem, and then the manifestos. Draw your own trajectories; arc the moment as you infer it from these contents. Underline a passage you like, and another and another—and also, we would presume, roll your eyes (perhaps less often).

Read a manifesto and write your own manifesto, and write the poems to mix or match. Read and write to change the world—because if you are writing to do anything other than that, if you are writing to the middle distance and not up to the stars, then you deserve the mediocrity you're creating and the status quo you're upholding.

A few words about the process. . . . When we first put out the call for entries to *The Manifesto Project*, we promised publicly that at least twenty-five percent of the volume's contents would consist of unsolicited submissions (so long as the submissions met our fundamental criterion, which was to have a book of poems in press or in print). As it turned out, more than fifty percent of the volume's contents are by poets who sent their work unsolicited. Writing a manifesto also means writing to be heard.

Editorially, both of us read all of the work submitted, over 115 entries, and collaborated on our selections as well as our edits. Some of the prose received edits; given that these are new works written explicitly for this volume, we felt authorized to ask the writers questions about their work. Notwithstanding, as editors, we yielded to our contributors: we remained cognizant of the volume's breadth, and that the contributors represent a range of ages, and present a range of aesthetics. No single way of reading characterizes *The Manifesto Project*'s contributors, nor may we assume the contents here constitute more than an historical moment. But what a moment—and what a concatenation of voices and art-attacks.

We have many people to thank for their hard work on this project. Each other . . . no, wait, that's not cool to say.

Let's try again:

We have many people to thank for helping make this book happen. Jessica Murray and Emi Moore, who provided indices, Mary Biddinger, Jon Miller, Amy Freels, and Carol Slatter of the University of Akron Press; Felicia van Bork; Mark Nathan Stafford; and the many poets and lovers of poetry who shared the call for submissions on social media.

More manifestos, please.
Alan Michael Parker & Rebecca Hazelton

Lisa Ampleman
There is Nothing New Under the Sun. Make it New.

There is nothing new, lamented a Jewish writer in third century B.C. "Even the thing of which we say, 'See, this is new!' has already existed in the ages that preceded us." He called himself Qoheleth, assembler or collector.

Later in the text, he says there's a time for everything, to give birth and to die. To weep and to laugh. "A time to cast away stones, and a time to gather stones together." He gathered his wisdoms, and twenty-two centuries later, Pete Seeger wrote a song from them, assembling the phrases word for word from the King James Bible. Fifteen years later, the Byrds made that song new, a number one hit. On rhythm guitar was David Crosby, whom my father later appreciated in his new role in Crosby, Stills, & Nash. I liked him as a pirate in the 1991 kids' movie *Hook*.

All this to say: Qoheleth had it right. There's plenty of wisdom out there to be found, and a student of poetry or a poet should read widely. Classical orators, Renaissance lyricists, French symbolists, Black Mountain poets, Tree-hugging-neoanarchists, etc. Even read those poets whose aesthetics jangle in your ear, whom you would never want to imitate. Be able to know how to read a formal poem if you like to experiment, or an experimental poem if you live for form. And read non-poetry too, to have content other than your own life and the subject of poetry itself. Research dragonfly sex, nephrology, investment banking.

During my MFA years, whenever I went to the university library, I ran into a classmate of mine. Sometimes he was revising a poem carefully and/or repeatedly ("Farflung Passion, draft 22," a file he emailed us might be named), but often he was reading. He would sit in the library for eight hours on a Saturday reading the collected Robert Lowell or the essays of T. S. Eliot or the chants of the medieval troubadours. He was voracious. He made every penny and every minute of his graduate degree count. And he became a better and better poet every year.

*

Make it new. A phrase that Pound found in Confucian texts and made new by putting it in the context of a manifesto. Or so we like to think. That phrase was never in a manifesto, however; it was only a title to a collection of essays and then snuck into a canto. It didn't become a "catchphrase" (Michael North's phrase) until the 1950s and '60s.

Like Bill Clinton parsing *is*, I must ask, what is *it*? In Pound's work, I've always thought that it's something like the Old, what we deem important from past cultures. One reason to be wary about such reliance on the past, as Louis Menand points out in the *New Yorker*, is that "to understand what Pound is doing you often need to have read the same writers, studied the same languages, and learned the same history that Pound read, studied, and learned (or rely on the commentary of a person who has)." The Old can be a monolithic, patriarchal, exclusionary space. So, find a new Old: do work with an ancient native language in decline, like Natalie Diaz. Remind us why the Civil Rights Movement of the '60s was necessary then and is still, like Jake Adams York, Roger Reeves, and more. The Old doesn't have to be the Old we're all used to.

In the end, your journeys in the Old act as counterpoint to your experiments in the New. During my doctoral studies, I spent an entire year reading more than 300 texts in preparation for my comprehensive exams. Those 300 texts included articles on critical theory, medieval romances, fat collected works, and slim but weighty volumes of contemporary poems. I didn't have time to write for most of that year because I had to read: on the bus to school, in the evening after dinner, at the beach on my honeymoon, on a trip to visit my family. I budgeted my time and became immersed especially in the courtly love tradition and its Petrarchan heirs in the Renaissance and beyond.

After I passed my exams, I was curious about Dante's wife, Gemma Donati; Anne Boleyn; Gaspara Stampa, a sixteenth-century Venetian who wrote a poetic sequence in the tradition of Petrarch; and Courtney Love, whose name sounded so close to the tradition. Their voices were there, and when I put in the time, I was able to explore those women's lives in comparative ease.

Thus, I firmly believe: When your writing is in a fallow season, read. Fill the well. When it's time to till again, you'll have water to irrigate, and crops aplenty.

And, young poet, experiment with forms; figure out what fits into the spaces and sounds demanded by the structure, whether sonnet or conceptual play. (But, dear god, be wary of sestinas and villanelles: Elizabeth Bishop ruined them for most of us by writing them so well. When you want to write a villanelle, read "One Art" and weigh whether your attempt can be as half as good. Or write that villanelle and set it aside for months, then see if it stands up. If not, scrap it for parts.)

Finally, try a new medium: Write a poem on your cell phone or as a Tweet. Speak into a voice recorder to compose. Make a short film to illustrate a finished draft. See what a poem looks like in a notebook, on a computer screen in a Word document, as hypertext on a website. Collaborate with other poets, artists, and musicians. Put your poems where they don't belong, guerrilla-style, and spread the news, of the old and the new.

The Old

Menand, Louis. "The Pound Error." *The New Yorker,* 9 June 2008, pp. 123–27.
North, Michael. "The Making of 'Make It New.'" *Guernica.* 15 August 2013.
    www.guernicamag.com/features/the-making-of-making-it-new/.

Paul and Fran

Noi leggiavamo un giorno per diletto
di Lancialotto come amor lo strinse . . .

We were reading one day for pleasure
of Lancelot and how love felled him . . .
—*Inferno*, Canto V

Reading a romance novel together
was the kindling, though they'd intended
to mock it, the stiffening members
and softening flesh. The hero tripped
and fell onto the couch, trapping
the sassy but stubborn lass under his
broad shoulders and muscled
chest. *I burn for you*, he said. And when
he kissed his woman, Paul did too,
though Fran was engaged to his brother.
Paperback tossed to the floor, they canoodled
on the futon. When Johnny heard, he bound them
together in the trunk and set the Chevy on fire.

But *romance* also means language,
so let's give them a reprieve, start the story
over. Paul reads Fran the dictionary instead.
They're on the pronunciation
guide. \ü\ as in *boudoir*, \ä\ as in *lingerie*.
She doesn't understand he's making a pass.
A couch dumped in front of her apartment
smolders, flame resistant material
refusing to combust. It will lie
out there, growing soggy with rain,
until the sanitation department
comes to haul it away.

from "Courtly Love"

(For Courtney Love)

IV. FIRST SIGHT
You were a wraith onstage;
Love's archer strung his bow
and socked me in the chest, handcuffed me to the cage
that would be my home. Whoso

list to hunt, I know a worthy prey:
you—your ice-blue eyes, bee-whine voice, honey hair.
But I was senseless, my sunburned brain
as useless as underwear.

Still, fainting I followed. I asked
to see you again—you said yes, then
didn't show. I offered you a flask
of whiskey, a needle (I'm sorry), myself (again).

You spurned me, your arms long and small.
Persistent, I committed to the freefall.

V. THE CLIFF OVER WAIKIKI
You wore pajamas to our wedding—
blue-checked—comfortable rara avis,
and after the vows, after the sunset kiss,
we both held pink flowers, shedding
those gender roles we hated.
I did don a gauzy gown, my hair
mussed by the wind. But I didn't care
about being the bride; I waited
for that other bird curled inside me
to be born. In our photos, my face
is solemn; you grin, aleatory prodigy.

We wouldn't celebrate our third anniversary—
I'd read your suicide note with its fucked-up grace,
to our gathered guests: lonely liturgy.

VII. BONDAGE

I loved a man as wrong as rain
as right as red paint,
as strict as whips and chains.
He was my nothingness,
my bodhisattva, my less
self-conscious-in-a-dress.

When I did the math,
we came out equal,
modern-rock miracle
queen of the riff-raff.
I was his S, I was his M.
My boy in layered sweaters
had me in velvet fetters
but sang himself a requiem.

VIII. HORSEMAN

You wound me, dear Sir, with your cornflower eyes
and your blonde-stringed hair and your two-toned
20-gauge shotgun. You bring me along
when you travel abroad, but that girl Death

finds you, singing, in Rome, gives you pill
after pill, tells you oblivion is better.
That harpy brings you a horse with fierce
gallop, and you suit up with saddle and spurs.

Lisa Ampleman

You ride to a greenhouse where the flowers
aren't potted yet and bury your fingers in humus.
And where is my bonny lad, and why aren't I
with him? And where is his steed and dear daughter?

You leave me a note under one flowerpot
to tell me the hell-hag was right.

Sandra Beasley
The Scientist Speaks

Ladies and gentlemen—Members of the Conservatory—I appreciate this invitation to join you. Let us begin with a brief historical review. Slide I, please:

WHEN I HEARD THE LEARN'D ASTRONOMER

When I heard the learn'd astronomer,
When the proofs, the figures, were ranged in columns before me,
When I was shown the charts and diagrams, to add, divide,
  and measure them,
When I sitting heard the astronomer where he lectured with
  much applause in the lecture-room,
How soon unaccountable I became tired and sick,
Till rising and gliding out I wander'd off by myself,
In the mystical moist night-air, and from time to time,
Look'd up in perfect silence at the stars.

—Walt Whitman (1819–1892)

Much has been made of poetry's inquiries into the sciences. We have before us Walt Whitman's "When I Heard the Learn'd Astronomer." We have, for additional consideration, such odes as Alan Shapiro's "Astronomy Lesson." Even William Wordsworth celebrated our evolving technologies with a sonnet entitled "Steamboats, Viaducts, and Railways." Poets envy the bright particulars of science. The academic vocabulary of chemistry is oft appropriated to describe romantic phenomenon, while contemporary verse is overrun with studies of capybara, platypi, and other zoological spectacles.

But what of science's inquiries into poetry?

Thus far, such inquiries have been driven by poets, not scientists. An example: in 1900, German physicist Max Planck announces the discovery of his constant, the basis for Quantum Theory. Subsequently, Mssrs. Yeats, Eliot, and Pound adopted the metaphors of "particles" and "waves" in pursuit of an irreducible quantum of poetry. They theorized such insight could revolutionize their craft.

But as scholar Daniel Albright describes, the love affair is tempestuous. By 1920, they villainized science for its encroachment on Modernist vision. Eliot populates "The Waste Land," with a sailor, a typist, and the blind and breasted Tiresias, yet not a single particle physicist.

Poet and physician William Carlos Williams would prove a better ally to science. His experimental *Kora in Hell*, and the colloquial *Spring and All,* had already marked a stylistic parting from Eliot, et al. "How can we accept Einstein's theory of relativity, affecting our very conception of the heavens about us of which poets write so much, without incorporating its essential fact—the relativity of measurements—into our own category of activity?" he asked. To channel this enthusiasm, he debuted his theory of the "variable foot." Alas, his foot stumbled en route to wider popularity.

As an inheritor to Dr. Williams's leanings, Charles Olson brought more scientific discipline to understanding craft than any poet before or since. Scholar Douglas Duhaime has articulated Olson's views in his fieldwork, including how Olson's Projective Verse moved Euclidean observations to non-Euclidean geometries while tackling the special theory of relativity ("spatial relations of words creates temporal relations in the text"). In another essay, Olson related Keats' negative capability to Heisenberg's Uncertainty Principle.

In writings on Robert Creeley, Olson organized poets in terms of their attention to gravitational or electromagnetic literary fields. As Duhaime notes, subsequent efforts to discuss Creeley's quantum mechanics for the sake of a unified field theory muddy things considerably. But Olson can hardly be blamed for getting bogged down in the same field as Albert Einstein himself. If there is one thing poets can learn from scientists, it is this: Any Grand Unified Theory is destined to fail.

There is no singular way in which poetry works, no one quality that makes a poem great. In attempting to define a poetics capacious enough to include all models, you will only lapse into generalities and platitudes about dice games.

 Yet there should be a coherent manner of describing poetic acts, a way to navigate what might seem a hollow abundance otherwise. As scientists, we were asked to make a meaningful inquiry using scientific methodology. No more loosey-goosey metaphors. No more "schools," which is the humanities' code for fitting patterns retroactively to data.

Like all experiments, we begin with a question:

> WHAT IS A POEM?

Our first duty is natural observation. A survey congregates around two apparent realities. One data set, observed on page or page-like structures, consists of what we have come to call "lineated" poems. The second data set, observed in settings such as schools, coffee shops, and bars, we took to calling "performative" poems.

Although these poems share a common attention to word choice, rhythm, and sound, they function in distinct manners. Though the first data set may be transmitted through oral performance, critical spatial characteristics—their *fixed* qualities—are lost. Though the second data set can be archived as text, some nuance of tone—their *dynamic* qualities—escapes.

We suspected it was not incidental that one modality of poetry is expressed in two dimensions, and another modality is expressed in three, each with their attendant conveniences and perils. Comparisons across modalities did not prove constructive.

Discussion of initial data leads us to formulate a theory: *There is a distinct dimensionality associated with each significant mode of poetic practice.*

Please cue Slide 3:

CASUAL VERNACULAR		DISTINGUISHING INTERPRETATION
2-D	"Page poems"	Fixed
3-D	"Stage poems"	Dynamic

To test this theory, we constructed a hypothesis. *If every poem operates in a defining dimensionality, with poetics correspondent to second- and third- dimensionalities, and our known dimensionalities include first and fourth dimension, there must be poems that uniquely occupy those dimensions as well.*

Could such a spectrum of poems be observed?

Experimental data for first-dimensionality of poems is recorded with relative ease. A colleague noticed an inconsistency in earlier observations from the wild: the "prose poem," which may be intended for textual settings but eschews line breaks. For purposes of taxonomy we term this an "unlineated" poetics. This is a slight misnomer, per the theories of Russell Edson, who was particularly attentive to the infinite potential of language as a vector; hence the frequent lapse into a closing ellipsis in his work, to resist the fallacy of an end-stopped line.

Fourth-dimensional poems initially proved elusive, with several failed attempts at observation. The "fourth dimension" is associated with the reconciliation of space and time. Though we considered pursuing examples of Olson's Projective Verse, any categorization that requires presumption of the author's knowledge is specious; also, his attention to time as a function of space was always expressed on the page, dictating his poems' second-dimensionality.

Affirming data eventually presented itself in the form of translation, which takes an existing poem and seeks to re-enact that poem in a different language and, *de facto*, a different time. Sometimes, the information accrued with the passage of time shades meaning. Few who translate from Miklós Radnóti's Bor notebook do so without knowing he died on the forced march through Hungary and Yugoslavia.

Other times, the passage of time shades craft. In his translation of *The Inferno*, Robert Pinsky acknowledges "In order to represent Dante's succinct, compressed quality along with the flow of *terza rima*, I have often found it necessary to write fewer lines in English than he uses in Italian." With this move, Pinsky acknowledges composition along the fourth dimensionality.

Let us pause to reflect:

DIMENSIONALITY	POETIC ACT
First	Unlineated
Second	Lineated
Third	Performative
Fourth	Translative

A strong theory must not only work with observational and experimental data, it must exhibit predictive qualities as well. Is this true of a Dimensional Theory of Poetics? Can considering extreme dimensionalities make a space for additional poetic acts?

Yes.

Please cue Slide 5:

THE ZERO-DIMENSIONAL POEM

If the zero dimension is a point, then in poetic terms it is a glut of word-matter generated in response to a prompt. Fluxists exhibit invitations to zero-dimensional work, per Yoko Ono's series of "Instructional Poems." Kenneth Goldsmith prescribes their assemblage from found resources, such as archival radio and television broadcasts.

Zero-dimension poems are, unfortunately, at the mercy of two-dimensional and three-dimensional delivery methods. If a zero-dimension poem could be hard-wired into consciousness, obviating cognitive hierarchies and distractions of syntax, the act would have even greater value than encounters in conventional reality.

Our task turns to the outer realms:

THE FIFTH-DIMENSIONAL POEM

The fifth dimension contains the sum outcomes generated by choices made in chance events across time. We borrow a term from chemistry, "multivalent," in which the ion sustains more than one valence potential on initial inspection.

The fifth-dimensional poem has been encountered in the field as the "erasure," made via inflection of an earlier text, in which the origin is disclosed as a critical component. Those looking for an exemplar might consult Mary Ruefle's *A Little White Shadow*, published in 2008, in tandem with its antecedent, Emily Malbone Morgan's "A Little White Shadow," originally published in 1890. Pleasure and meaning is derived only after considering the totality of available choices. The poem is defined not only by what is present, but by what is absent. Other forms may exist as well.

Our team has decided to call this the "Dimensional Theory of Poetics." Though there are other qualitative ways to discuss poetry, this system has proven both comprehensive and illuminating—leading us to relevant data that might have otherwise gone unobserved. Dimensional Theory recognizes the heterogeneous challenges that arise with poetic acts, without the denigrating implication that certain acts are not "really" poems, or that their practitioners are not "really" poets.

Acknowledging poetry's operant realities, in their full diversity, girds critical discussion of individual acts by framing the appropriate poems of comparison, and clarifying the dimensional goals.

To summarize:

DIMENSIONALITY	POETIC ACT
Zero	Conceptual
First	Unlineated
Second	Lineated
Third	Performative
Fourth	Translative
Fifth	Multivalent

This is an exciting time in the field. Will we someday speak of a ninth-dimensional poem? A tenth-dimensional poem? Although it is difficult to conceptualize dimensions six and higher in practical terms, we have models from superstring theory—such as the Calabi-Yau manifold, which can generate mirror symmetry—that may prove productive. The full ramifications of Dimensional Theory remain to be seen.

Thank you. And with that, I yield to your questions.

Works Cited

Albright, Daniel. *Quantum Poetics: Yeats, Pound, Eliot, and the Science of Modernism*. Cambridge UP, 1997.

Duhaime, Douglas. "Charles Olson and the Quest for a Quantum Poetics." Dissertation, University of Wisconsin-Milwaukee, 2014.

Pinsky, Robert, translator. *The Inferno of Dante: A New Verse Translation, Bilingual Edition*. By Dante, Farrah, Straus & Giroux, 1996.

Whitman, Walt. "When I Heard the Learn'd Astronomer." *Leaves of Grass*, self-published, 1865.

Williams, William Carlos. "The Poem as a Field of Action." *Selected Essays*. New Directions, 1969.

The Sand Speaks

I'm fluid and omnivorous, the casual
kiss. I'll knock up your oysters.
I'll eat your diamonds. I'm a mutt, no
one thing at all, just the size that counts

and if you're animal small enough, come;
if you're vegetable small enough, come;
if you're mineral small enough, come.
Mothers, brush me from the hands

of your children. Lovers, shake me
from the cuffs of your pants. Draw
a line, make it my mouth: I'll name
your country. I'm a Yes man at heart.

Let's play Hide and Go Drown. Let's play
Pearls for His Eyes. When the men fall
I like the way their arms touch, their legs
touch. There are always more men, men

who bring bags big enough to hold
each other. A man who kneels down
with a smaller bag, cups and pours, cups
and pours, as if I could prove anything.

Sandra Beasley

Let Me Count the Waves

> We must not look for poetry in poems.
> —Donald Revell

You must not skirt the issue wearing skirts.
You must not duck the bullet using ducks.
You must not face the music with your face.
Headbutting, don't use your head. Or your butt.
You must not use a house to build a home,
and never look for poetry in poems.

In fact, inject giraffes into your poems.
Let loose the circus monkeys in their skirts.
Explain the nest of wood is not a home
at all, but a blind for shooting wild ducks.
Grab the shotgun by its metrical butt;
aim at your Muse's quacking, Pringled face.

It's good we're talking like this, face to face.
There should be more headbutting over poems.
Citing an '80s brand has its cost but
honors the teenage me, always in skirts,
showing my sister how to Be the Duck
with a potato-chip beak. Take me home,

Mr. Revell. Or make yourself at home
in my postbellum, Reconstruction face—
my gray eyes, my rebel ears, all my ducks
in the row of a defeated mouth. Poems
were once civil. But war has torn my skirts
off at the first ruffle, baring my butt

or as termed in verse, my luminous butt.
Whitman once made a hospital his home.
Emily built a prison of her skirts.
Tigers roamed the sad veldt of Stevens's face.
That was the old landscape. All the new poems
map the two dimensions of cartoon ducks.

We're young and green. We're braces of mallards,
not barrels of fish. Shoot if you must but
Donald, we're with you. Trying to save poems,
we settle and frame their ramshackle homes.
What is form? Building art from artifice,
trading pelts for a more durable skirt.

Even urban ducklings deserve a home.
Make way. In the modern: *Make way, Buttface.*
A poem's coming through, lifting her skirt.

Sean Bishop
Slow Poetry

This manifesto begins with a story about two prior manifestos, written by two men separated by their art forms, by four thousand miles, and by their native languages. One was an Italian food critic. The other was an American poet. Neither man knew the other, but each had a profound influence on his field through a shared, ridiculous, beautiful hatred. A hatred for Ronald McDonald.

It was 1983, birth year of the McNugget. The food critic was Carlo Petrini, who that year created a non-profit food-and-wine association called Arcigolo, which shortly thereafter protested the opening of a McDonald's in Rome. Arcigolo's objections to McDonald's were about what you'd expect as a twenty-first century North American who has seen *Super Size Me*: it lamented the globalized interchangeability of low-quality, irresponsibly produced, non-nutritious food. A few years later, Petrini's Arcigolo group became Slow Food, an international organization and movement dedicated to "good, clean, and fair" food production and consumption. Thirty years after its founding, that movement is ubiquitous; it seems no self-respecting chef or food critic can ignore the cause.

The other man in question was Donald Hall, future poet laureate of the United States, who in 1983 published the essay "Poetry and Ambition," sometimes known as "the McPoem essay." Anytime anyone accuses MFA programs of churning out "too many poets" who in turn spit forth a glut of interchangeable "workshop poems," he or she is calling back to Hall's essay, or at least unknowingly reiterating it. Hall called the products of the MFA factory system "McPoems," and he encouraged young poets to stop focusing on production and publication and to strive instead for a place in literary history, emulating the "great ones" (who were, *oops*, all white and mostly cis-male.)

But Hall's manifesto did more than create the discourse surrounding poetic mass-production in the United States, it also flash-froze that discourse. For three decades, it seems, the discussion has been reduced to good/bad, either/or binaries: Are there "too many poets," or not? Are MFA programs good for literature, or not? Does American poetry suffer from sameness, or not? Does "MFA" or "NYC" hold the future for American literature? Such questions are defeated not even by their content so much as by their own rhetorical structures. The obvious answer is always "*both!*," but "both" needs to be the beginning of our conversation, not the end.

If I sound dismissive of Donald Hall, here, please know that I'm really not: for all its institutionalized racism, elitist poo-pooing, and over-sardonic metaphorizing, "Poetry and Ambition" was remarkably prescient, at least insofar as it predicted three fundamental changes to the poetic landscape: (1) The number of hopeful "professional" poets really has exploded since Hall's essay, by a factor of five to fifteen, depending on whose statistics you trust. (2) The MFA really has become the default, expected path by which hopefuls try to "become a poet" (whatever that means). And (3) as any seasoned editor of a consistently successful journal could tell you, as a group these new, numerous, MFA-bred poets are submitting more poems, more often, to more journals than their forebears did. Regular and widespread publication is a high priority for them.

So why even bother with Slow Food in this manifesto? Well, because unlike the McPoem discourse, Slow Food's focus shifted very quickly from attacking McDonald's to accepting the reality of fast food, and using some of the same global communications and marketing networks that had created McDonald's in the first place to formulate an alternative that could coexist *beside* McDonald's—Slow Food realized it didn't need to destroy fast food to succeed.

As members of the poetry community, we need to stop fighting over the imagined implications of unchangeable facts, and instead start talking positively about "Slow Poetry" as a constructive effort that everyone can get behind or tip their hats to, regardless of whether they think the culture of "fast poetry" is a threat or even a real thing. Because in the end, even if some among us *do* think there are "too many poets" writing interchangeable, semi-autobiographical "workshop poems," what are we going to do about it? Kill them off? Shame them until they quit writing? Obviously these aren't realistic or reasonable—or least of all *desirable*—options.

Whether or not we care about Slow Food, we can learn from it. For my own sake, I can say that as I write this, I am literally eating a "dinner" of chili-cheese Fritos and beer. I enjoy a good farm-to-table meal as much as the next guy, but I also love a grease-laden twenty-sack of McNugs, served with a Coke the size of my bathroom trashcan. My point here is about *poetry*, in the end, not food.

GOOD, CLEAN, AND FAIR

These are the keywords of the Slow Food manifesto. "Good" meaning "quality, flavorsome and healthy food." "Clean" meaning the food production and consumption doesn't hurt the environment. And "Fair" meaning nobody's getting gouged, price-wise, from farming to preparation to consumption. How could these three keywords unite disparate poetic movements under a diverse but unified set of objectives? What would these criteria even *mean*, in the American poetic context?

GOOD: Goodness is easily the most controversial and unwieldy of our criteria, so let's just start by acknowledging, yes, we've all read *Zen and the Art of Motorcycle Maintenance*, we know the sound of one hand clapping, we know that "quality" and "goodness" have no objective reality. Rather, we should proceed from the understanding that goodness is something we all make and define together over time, as producers, editors, teachers, critics, and consumers of poetry. It is by nature wrapped up in our ever-shifting social context, and so it's constantly under revision. Okay? Okay.

With that out of the way, it's still impossible to evaluate the goodness of our immediate poetic moment, because we're standing in the middle of it and we can't get the perspective we need to see its shape. But we know for sure that the *quantity* of poets and poems has exploded. And while on the one hand we can agree that the quality-versus-quantity binary is yet another false piece of rhetoric, on the other hand we can acknowledge that if a poet is constantly trying to get his or her next poem "finished" and submitted, he or she may spend less time mulling each poem over. This means the poet is not as likely to question each poem's underlying ambitions and assumptions as thoroughly as he or she might otherwise, or to question what (if anything) the poem is adding to the world (in terms of "flavor" or "health," if you want to stretch our Slow Food conceit to its limits). The more focused we are on getting the next poem written, the less time we spend evaluating poetry written by ourselves and others, and as a result our criteria for goodness become less clear, meaningful, and useful.

We can't say for certain that speed and quantity have resulted in worse poetry being published, but we can concede that they potentially put goodness at risk, as a value and a goal. Furthermore, the sheer number of poets and poetry publishers, combined with our increasingly foggy understanding of poetic quality, means that even if there are more good poets, editors, readers than there ever have been in America, that goodness becomes more difficult to find in the massive clutter of production. Finally, prioritizing or even *praising* quantity and speed puts long-form, research-driven, and formally complicated poetry projects at a disadvantage; writing those kinds of poems and books simply requires harder work over a longer period of time.

In the warming, infra-red lamp-light of these observations, the question becomes, how do we make goodness more of a priority? Some of us might think that judging goodness—judging *anything*—needn't and shouldn't be a priority for poets at all, because over time the best poems will rise to the top, yes? And it's just the poet's job to write, right? Let the editors and readers decide what's best! I don't have the space to engage fully with this counter-argument except to say that it's simultaneously over-trusting of and disrespectful toward editors and readers, and that there is no measurable evidence at all to suggest that what gets anthologized and canonized is actually what's "best." Anecdotally, I can say I certainly don't feel that way when I read the *Best American* or *Pushcart* anthologies, or especially any of the now-extant *Contemporary American Poetry* anthologies. And I feel even less certain that the best writing is by nature the writing that will be remembered and praised when, at the bar after a reading, I eavesdrop on other attendees' conversations, which tend to revolve around the poets who have the largest Twitter and Facebook presences, and who have said or done the most outlandish or controversial things recently.

But back to the goal of goodness. For poets, I think the first step is to believe that one's goodness as a poet has little or nothing to do with whether one finished a poem in a particular week or month or even year. Poets need to become more comfortable throwing away most of what they have written, more comfortable abandoning unfinished poems, and most importantly more comfortable *not writing* in the first place. To say this, nowadays, may seem like an absurdity. It has become common for teachers to tell their students to treat writing poems like a job, and while this can be productive for undergraduates who are still learning some basic elements of craft that have little or nothing to do with poetic content or ambition, it is idiotic advice to post-graduate students and even many current MFA candidates, who should be concerned primarily with making or communicating something of artistic and social value. If you treat writing poems as putting-some-words-on-the-page-today-because-that's-your-job, then words-on-the-page-today will start to become what poetry means to you.

This attitude hurts poetry as well as the poet—much more so than the admittedly snooty and precious idea of "waiting for the Muse"—because nobody on this planet has something urgent and worthy of being said every day, or even every week or every month. We need to learn to have faith that we will, eventually, have something important to communicate as poets, that even in the midst of prolonged silences we continue to *be* poets, and that by keeping silent and listening when we don't have something important to say, we create a space where the poets who do can be heard. At the moment, for most poets under forty and even many mid-to-late-career poets, it's as if we are worried that if we stop publishing even for a moment, if we stop seeing ourselves in magazines, we will cease to exist. That attitude doesn't help anyone who holds it, and it *certainly* doesn't help poetry as a whole. To indulge Donald Hall's snarky metaphor: we do not need to maintain, at all times, a new bunch of poems wrapped in foil, sitting on the steam shelf, above the fryolator. We don't need to be open twenty-four hours.

To prioritize goodness above all else, as a poet, means only submitting to magazines the poems that you believe to be great and important and that the world needs to read. It means, when putting together a book manuscript, omitting those poems that were published in prestigious magazines but that you do not feel any longer are great, important poems. And just as importantly, it means *including* the poems that you still believe are great and important even if no magazine ever validated them through publication. It means having profound respect for and trust in yourself while maintaining even more respect for the editors and readers who will encounter your work. If you don't think a particular poem urgently *needs* to be read, why would you think anyone else should spend time with it? As a poet, striving toward goodness also means holding magazines and presses accountable. It means reading the poems and books published by those presses, and regardless of their perceived reputations, refusing to submit to them if you believe they are not publishing work of consistently high quality. Similarly and more importantly, it means assessing lesser-known magazines and presses, and if you think they're publishing a lot of exciting and meaningful work, sending them your best stuff even if you have no sense of their reputations.

Which brings us to "goodness" as a reader, as a poetry-eater or consumer. More than anything, being a good reader means reading a *lot*, and thinking about presses and publishers as creators in their own rights. Being a good reader also means being very loud about work you encounter and love, regardless of whether the writer of that work is "taggable" or a "friend" or a "follower" or is reachable to you or anyone else via social media at all. On the flip side, it means getting Amish on poets who receive more attention than they deserve: *shunning* them rather than throwing shade at them in public forums, which only exacerbates the problem and communicates that—good or bad—the poet in question is worthy of discussion.

And finally there's "goodness" for the poetry-chefs; for the editors (because poets are the farmers in this overburdened conceit, remember?). Just "good" should never, ever be good *enough* to warrant publication; any editor worth his or her salt should be rejecting a large quantity of work that he or she sincerely and wholeheartedly loves, in favor of work that is not only sincerely loved but that also has the most important thing to say or do in our cultural moment. If it ever becomes necessary to publish work that is just "good," an editor either needs to take drastic actions to improve his or her magazine/press, or embrace failure and shut down out of respect for the community. Furthermore, editors should be abnormally dedicated readers, as outlined above, and should strive to solicit work not from the poets who will garner attention for the magazine, but from the poets they believe to be best regardless of career or fame. Especially now that online publishing makes it cheap and easy to publish anything and everything, and digital printing can make even book-publishing a reasonable expense, editors need to take it upon themselves to enforce much stricter standards. The market pressures that used to enforce selectiveness, among editors—*i.e.* money, *i.e.* "production costs"—barely exist anymore. Now we have to respect selectiveness itself as one of our highest priorities, as painful and laborious as that may be.

[CLEAN] **COMMUNITY FOCUSED:** In Slow Food International's official statement of philosophy, which touts the three pillars of "good, clean, and fair," "clean" is paraphrased to mean "production that does not harm the environment." To translate this concept of cleanliness for Slow Poetry would risk accusing certain poetics of having poisonous effects on the literary environment, which (true or not) won't help us to correct the crippling negativity and reactionism that has defined the McPoem discourse. So let's not go there. Instead, let's focus on a heavily implied element of "cleanliness" for the Slow Food movement—the use of locally produced food and regional culinary traditions—and how this focus generates a sense of regional community that strengthens the movement even further.

We need to answer two questions here: what would "community focus" look like for Slow Poetry? And how or why is it desirable? For poets, editors, teachers, and readers alike, focusing on community would mean spending more time engaging with other poets, editors, and readers in one's immediate vicinity—in book groups, in non-hierarchal workshops, in classes at public libraries, at readings, in the offices of local publishers, in bars, in cafés—than one spends actually sitting down to write poems, or engaging with non-local publishers and writers. It means shifting one's perception so that writing poems is just one small piece of being a poet, and paradoxically not even the largest or most important piece, because to write and publish poems holds little or no meaning if one does not first have a community that values the poetry one writes. We don't have a *right* to that community, we have a responsibility to *create* it. So if book clubs, publishers, workshops, and readings don't exist in one's community, then "community focus" means making those resources from scratch. And if a poet lives in a Winesburgian nowhereland for poetry, where no amount of effort could create a community, "community focus" means doing what one has to do to escape that environment for the nearest cultural center (*á la* George Willard), or it means using the same social networking applications I whined about a few paragraphs ago to cultivate such a community virtually . . . not just a bunch of Facebook "friends" whose posts you "like," but a community to whom you feel all the obligation and commitment you would feel to the actual physical people you see every day. For most of us, if we spent as much time engaging meaningfully with our immediate literary communities as we do the vague mass of writers whose names we sort of recognize on Twitter and Facebook, we would be much more content with ourselves as poets, and American poetry would be better off.

But that brings us to the "why." I can think of at least three good reasons. First, focusing on our immediate communities will ameliorate some of the anxieties and self-doubts that cause poets to overproduce, over-submit, and over-publish in the first place. When we feel validated and valued as poets by the people that surround us, we will feel less compulsion to over-produce and over-publish as a way of being validated by anonymous figures whose support is, at best, only abstractly satisfying.

It should be obvious that the existing community structures of "literary" poetry are alienating: In literal communities like New York, with the rapid turnover of huge swaths of young ambitious poets who are just barely surviving for a while before falling off and burning out, it's hard for any poet not to see the faces in the crowd as "petals on a wet, black bough." One not only detaches emotionally from the masses of fresh new faces passing through (Why invest or get attached? They'll be gone soon.), but also becomes hyper-vigilant about trying to "succeed" so as not to be among the failures and losses. It's no way to live.

The MFA system is even worse: groups of strangers are brought together from all over the country, for two years of intensive camaraderie and collaboration, and then scattered back into the landscape where (more often than not) they quickly lose touch with one another. All that they are able to keep, from that magical two-or-three-year whirlwind of artistic validation and patronage, is the only thing over which they always had complete control: their own writing. And so they let the writing swell and fester, becoming their near-total definition of what it means to be a poet. They take pride in the obsessive be-all and end-all of it. They try desperately to publish publish publish, not only because the acceptance letters and magazines that arrive in the mail help them believe for a brief moment that they really are poets, that those few years of validation and patronage were not just a dream, but also because publishing seems their best hope of getting back into the academic institution where poetry felt *real* for those two or three years, this time as professors rather than students.

I'm speaking generally and hyperbolically here, of course. Not all young or younger poets fit the description above, but many do. And when you look back at some of the most famous, successful literary communities—for instance the Lake Poets, the Transcendentalists in New Hampshire and Massachusetts, or the Harlem Renaissance—it's worth recognizing that these were for the most part regional communities where many of the poets ate and drank and pissed and shit and fucked and got married and divorced and lived and died, *together*. The members of these communities had each other as near-constant mutual presences; they were one another's friends, editors, critics, and colleagues; they collaborated with and validated one another even during periods of creative dearth. It's hard to imagine a figure like Coleridge succeeding today, who went through long bouts of not-writing, and two of whose most famous poems were left completely unfinished not because Coleridge died while writing them, but just because he didn't finish them. Being a poet—at least being a Lake Poet—wasn't first and foremost about producing a constant stream of tidy, finished poems, it was about having long talks and arguing and trying to figure out, with his neighbors, what the future of poetry should be.

The list of influential poetry communities, above, brings us to the second way that a focus on regional community benefits American poetry. If we stop trying to pretend we can listen to and respond to everyone, and focus instead on the poetic values, beliefs, and projects immediately surrounding us, I think we will find that the overall noise and din of the poetry population explosion becomes much more manageable and much less anxiety-producing. We shouldn't *strive* for ignorance of a national or international context, obviously. But one does not need to be talking with, or listening to, the entire English-speaking poetry world to become one of the most important figures in that world. The Harlem Renaissance is a beautiful case in point. Of course there were social and political factors (to make a coy and profound understatement) that kept the poets of the Harlem Renaissance from engaging as much with the "larger" (or, um, whiter) poetic world as they otherwise might have, but it's remarkable to note that even immensely successful and universally anthologized poets of the movement were primarily focused on and centered in Harlem long after they achieved national and international success. They didn't run away, once they were successful, and take part instead in some elitist conversation about "American Poetry." American Poetry, for many of them, *was* the Harlem Renaissance. This was even true for Countee Cullen, the most famous poet of the movement apart from Hughes, who published early poems in mainstream magazines like *Harper's* and *Poetry* but published a much more substantial percentage of his work in black arts journals like *Opportunity*, *The Crisis*, and *The Messenger*.

What the examples of the Lake Poets, the Transcendentalists, and the Harlem Renaissance illustrate is something that anyone who has visited Australia or the Galapagos archipelago already knows: diversity is a product of relative autonomy, and in extreme cases, of isolation. The same is true, aesthetically, in the arts. If we all focus more on the conversations, convictions, and aesthetics in our immediate communities, and spend a little less time trying to keep tabs on capital-A, capital-P American Poetry—which has grown too large to keep tabs on, anyway—we will see greater creative diversity. We may even start to regard the broad idea of "American Poetry" with roughly the same amount of seriousness as we regard the "American Fare" advertised by mall-adjacent restaurant chains.

One last, brief argument in favor of community focus: when we prioritize our immediate literary communities, we make ourselves more visible and relatable to non-poets and to poets outside of the MFA system; we expand the audience and the general appreciation for poetry. If you live in a city with public transportation, you have probably seen the godawful trash that often passes for "public poetry," sitting alongside the advertisements inside buses and trains. Why aren't we, as actual poets, doing something about that? Why aren't we trying to make sure poetry—*good* poetry—is included in every local festival or community event? When we stay locked up in our Universities, or we engage with poetry only through reading and writing and publishing, we allow an idea of poetry to circulate that makes the art form even less desirable to the larger world. We let the world continue to think that poetry is either sentimental musings about flowers and birds and love and loneliness, or incomprehensible jargon penned by professors in ivory towers. But if we get out there—even if that just means having audible conversations about poetry in public places like cafés and bars—people outside of ourselves might take more interest in what we're doing.

FAIR: When it comes to money, fairness is pretty simple, in poetry. It's simple because—sadly—there's very little money in poetry to begin with. Poetry is a patronage economy, or maybe if you want to be very optimistic about it, a gift economy: what money there is, if you follow it far enough, comes from wealthy individuals and corporations (*e.g.* Ruth Lilly, Target, the Guggenheim Foundation) or from the government (*e.g.* the National Endowment for the Arts, state-funded universities). The paying readership constitutes a very distant third source of poetry funding. Though it's tempting to see magazines and presses as businesses, poets and poetry readers should be aware that most editors work as volunteers, or for meager stipends, or at the very most for a reasonable, livable wage. The only people who are perhaps getting richer than they deserve, from poetry, are doing so through the generosity of colleges and universities who believe that having a prestigious artist on campus is a worthwhile and valuable thing. Those institutions aren't exactly deserving of attack, even if we do wish they'd spread the money around to other poets. After all, we *want* a world where great writers can live comfortably.

So to the extent that "fairness" should be a goal for Slow Poetry, it isn't so much a monetary goal. We can do some small things, though, to help each other out:

(1) Poets should not submit to presses or magazines that charge general submission fees. Ever. Such publishers don't deserve to exist. Contest fees, of course, are another story: contest fees are voluntary and are the main means by which many presses and journals that lack grant funding cover basic operating costs, while at the same time giving most of the fees back to the contest winners. So publishers shouldn't be derided for holding contests unless it's clear they are raking in a lot more money, in fees, than they are putting back into the press itself and into the winners' pockets.

(2) Poets should not submit to any magazine or press that pays its editors but does not pay its contributors; any respectable editor will prioritize production costs first (which are sizable, believe me), and contributor compensation second. Only after those goals are accomplished should an editor provide a stipend to him or herself.

(3) Readers should pay for poetry, whenever they can. We do ourselves a disservice by expecting poetry to be free. We should buy books, and whenever possible we should buy those books directly from the small presses that publish them, or from independent bookstores. None of us, under any circumstances, should be buying books from Amazon that we could buy by other means; the money we'll save just isn't worth the damage we'll be doing to the poetry community. When it comes to literary jour-

nals, especially now that so much publishing happens online and is accessible to everyone free of charge, readers should do what they can to donate to those magazines. And many print-magazines give free subscriptions to contest entrants, which is a very fair deal—*better* than fair.

(4) The above applies to readings, as well: poetry readings are almost always free to attend. But giving a reading is never free—there are travel costs, there are volunteers organizing the reading, there is usually a bookstore or a café or a bar that has donated its space. Whenever possible, if you're attending readings, you should be buying the poet's books, donating to the series, and patronizing the business hosting the event.

But fairness is bigger than money. At the end of the day, fairness is generosity; we need to be good to each other. We need to give everyone the best chance we can. We need to strive for equality, of race and gender and social class, of age and generation, and of aesthetic. We need to focus on our own communities yet remain open to others, open to anyone who wants to join our clubs. We don't gain anything by shutting people out, regardless of whether there are "too many poets." We've all given ourselves over to an art form that is underappreciated and funded almost totally through generous patrons, and we've all done it for the same reason: because we love it. A spirit of debate is great—I've been going at it for five thousand words now—but the resentment and naysaying that dominates so much of the poetry discourse just has to stop.

WHO CARES WHAT WE CALL IT?

A lot of what I've discussed here goes by other names or has been a part of other efforts: "Literary Citizenship," for instance. Or the movement, in classrooms, to champion process over product, quality over quantity. Or the general rumblings and grumblings against Amazon that have not (so far) translated into a positive movement in support of small bookstores and presses. It has been my goal, in this manifesto, to show how these various efforts might be understood as integrated pieces of a larger framework called Slow Poetry, modeled on the Slow Food movement. Slow Poetry attempts to reprioritize "goodness" and quality in poetry-writing and publishing, to make "poet" mean more than "producer of poems," and to reinvigorate the American poetic landscape by re-instilling in poets a sense of their own belonging and validity as artists within their own regional and aesthetic communities.

But when push comes to shove, I really don't care if it's called Slow Poetry. I haven't registered slowpoetry.org, though last I checked it's available. Because I mean, really: "Slow Poetry?" It's kind of derivative, isn't it? We can come up with a better name. We can come up with other models, as good as or better than Slow Food. This whole manifesto is just meant to begin a conversation, really, to try to rally us poets behind something positive for a change. I'll be interested to see if anything comes of it, if anyone wants to push this thing a step further. And if anyone does, you know where to find me: I'll be at McDonald's. I hear they've got this new thing—mostly corn syrup, probably, and that red dye that's made from crushed-up beetles—called the Cherry Berry Chiller.

Works Cited

Anderson, Sherwood, and Ray Lewis White. *Sherwood Anderson's Winesburg, Ohio: with variant readings and annotations*. Ohio University Press, 1997.

"Carlo Petrini." *Wikipedia*. en.wikipedia.org/wiki/Carlo_Petrini. Accessed August 10, 2014.

"Chicken McNuggets." *Wikipedia*. en.wikipedia.org/wiki/Chicken_McNuggets. Accessed August 10, 2014.

Early, Gerald and Clifton H. Johnson. "Countee Cullen." *Modern American Poetry*. www.english.illinois.edu/maps/poets/a_f/cullen/life.htm. Accessed August 10, 2014.

Hall, Donald. "Poetry and Ambition." *poets.org*. www.poets.org/poetsorg/text/poetry-and-ambition. Accessed August 10, 2014.

Harbach, Chad, ed. *MFA vs NYC: The Two Cultures of American Fiction*. Faber and Faber, 2014.

Pirsig, Robert M. *Zen and the art of motorcycle maintenance: an inquiry into values*. Morrow, 1974.

"Samuel Taylor Coleridge." *Wikipedia*. en.wikipedia.org/wiki/Samuel_Taylor_Coleridge. Accessed August 10, 2014.

"Slow Food: Our Philosophy." *Slow Food*. www.slowfood.com/about-us/our-philosophy/. Accessed August 10, 2014.

Spurlock, Morgan. *Super Size Me*. Hart Sharp Video, 2004.

GENECIES

The
heart
is

such
a   simple

fruit,   so   small
and

slow

to

sing,

a
hive

for   a

love
as

constructed

and

imaginary
as

the excavation of

Genesis.

Speak of a

passage.

Speak of

a
form.

Speak of

a picture

of the world

worth notice

to become a
subject for

proofs
or

florists'
drawings:

a handful of feathers

in the
tree,

like

a
suit the soil

owed to

the
thrush.

I will not   here give a

suspect   so

useless

as

hell,

the
prehensile

waste

a
snake

is a sign of,

a
domestic animal

as

enduring

as

certain
fruit-trees

in
Jerusalem.

But if Man
will be
a tree,
if
his seed were
lace,

if

the young

will

swarm

in a future

as

clear

as

mown turf,

at least

we have

our

enemies,

in

winter,

to get

some
times

in   struggle

touched by

a
remarkable

heat.

War

is often required
to be

near each other,

in
a
garden

so
plain

and
perfect

and

vast;

a
broken
future we

suffer

and leave,

to return to

the earth

exposed

as   a
less perfect   animal.

We
destroy.

We
subsist.

We travel

and

we travel   and

we travel

and

we reach the

snow-capped

end.

Susan Briante
Big Data Birdsong

A red-eyed vireo sings more than 20,000 songs a day. The brown thrasher sings 2,000 distinct songs. Some birds winnow, others like the Gila woodpecker drum.

A wildlife biologist recently told me that at one time he could recognize more than 200 distinct birdcalls. He trained himself in this identification with sound recordings and flash cards.

Now the biologist is earning his PhD in statistics writing articles such as "Population status distribution and effects of fires on buff breasted flycatchers" or "The influences of water quality on the health of the riparian bird community in Arizona."

As is often the case for the poet, song led him to data.

There is more data available to the poet than ever before, and I find this material both inspiring as well as difficult. We live at a time when every log-in and every purchase made, as well as each text, email, or photo sent, becomes tangled in a very large net formed by ubiquitous information-sensing mobile devices, aerial sensory technologies, software logs, cameras, microphones, radio-frequency identification readers, and wireless sensor networks. A student of data collection and national security websites tells me every keystroke we enter into our email or phone gets recorded at least eight times. All of this is stockpiled by governments and corporations, a Katrina-like rising tide of big data.

We live in a world of big data, although I'm not even sure that is the right name for it.[1]

In this swarm of uncontextualized information, we need to ask the questions: Who controls and who sees such data? Whose stories are privileged and whose are silenced? What narratives are being made up about us?

While the downsides of this data collection are documented in books such as Julia Angwin's *Dragnet Nation*, I wonder about what possibilities this data holds for the poet.

You can listen to hundreds of bird songs on your laptop or smart phone.

In her 1982 collection *Midwinter Day*, Bernadette Mayer writes "an epic poem about a daily routine" (Alice Notley) chronicling twenty four hours in her life in sections that move from dream to morning to afternoon to evening and back to dream. Mayer explains: " I had the idea to write a book that would translate the detail of thought from a day to language . . . because having it all at once is performing a magical service for survival." How could Mayer's inquiry be expanded upon today?

Angwin said that reading her extended Google search history was like "reading her own mind."

Know thyself, the Oracle said.

Know thy carbon footprint via the Nature Conservancy Carbon Footprint Calculator, thy genealogy via ancestry.com

The poet types the words "Track your" into a Google search and finds:

Track your happiness (www.trackyourhappiness.org)
Tracking UPS
Track your hours
Track your child, elderly, pets or possessions
Track your Fed-Ex
Track your plaque heart disease reversal

This knowledge can work in service of a broad poetic project. This knowledge need not be narcissistic. The novelist writing about physics says: "Any description of the universe is a description of the instrument used to take your reading" (Wilson).

The poet can know herself as instrument, can learn the ways in which she is both as complicit in and resistant to late capitalism. The poet can put personal anecdote in the service of broader investigations, can see her own experiences and perceptions as another piece of data within a larger inquiry. As Shelley reminds us, the poet can behold "intensely the present as it is, and discover those laws according to which present things ought to be ordered."

The poet can see herself as more than credit score.

Big data helps the traders on Wall Street make money algorithmically between the seconds across the date lines. But somewhere, too, scientists use big data to look for the "god" particle.

Like the physicist, the poet can turn to data to find the most elemental information about herself and her world, tracing the intersections between individuals and systems, charting our connections and complicities, attuned to easy narratives set like traps, as well as the stories erased or unrecorded in all of this monitoring.

The poet should not NSA, collecting data without context, but perhaps the poet can train her sights like a Google street view reading her environment, opening the viewfinder with an awareness of larger cartographies.

Perhaps in some way this data can help us bear witness to the blood-soaked and beautiful present.

Tracking birds in the Sonora desert, the biologist often came across immigrants wandering scared, separated from guides and families. He said he learned to carry more water and move more gently.

Perhaps, like the wildlife biologist, the poet can learn to carry more water and move gently.

A version of this essay was presented at Naropa University in June 2014 as part of a week devoted to Documentary Poetics during the Summer Writing Program.

Notes

1. Adelaide Morris writing about Gertrude Stein's insistent phrase "but everybody knows that" reminds us that Stein was pointing to the "lag between two kinds of knowledge: what we know because it is what we see or do and what we know because it is what we think" (Morris 1). The first documented cases of PTSD described anxiety disorders suffered as a result of early passenger train accidents and were known at the time as "railway spine." Thinking and naming dawdles behind us like the automobile engine we measure in horsepower.

Works Cited

Angwin, Julia. *Dragnet Nation: A Quest for Privacy, Security, and Freedom in a World of Relentless Surveillance*. Times Books, 2014.

Mayer, Bernadette. *Midwinter Day*. New Directions, 1999.

Morris, Adelaide. "New Media Poetics: As We May Think/How to Write." *New Media Poetics: Contexts, Technotexts, and Theories*. Edited by Adelaide Morris and Thomas Swiss, MIT Press, 2009, pp. 1–46.

Shelley, Percy Bysshe. "A Defense of Poetry." *The Poetry Foundation*. 13 October 2009. www.poetryfoundation.org/resources/learning/essays/detail/69388.

Wilson, Robert Anton. "Quantum Physics Explained, Simply." *YouTube*. 27 May 2009. www.youtube.com/watch?v=cEl-fTtP2tw.

The Market as Composition

On February 10, 10:04 in the morning, the Dow falls to 12194. Who swims? Who rafts or islands? Rivers rise like the Southern Pacific Railroad Company. Characters ticker between us; characters leaf. Both the river and its banks are moving

past a grove of southern trees. Mimosa, magnolia, Osage orange. Our indexing makes trails through a forest of mind. Hot linked, jumpy. On the day William Carlos Williams died the Dow closed up 667. Branches

scrawl across a winter white sky. Black branch, yellow leaf. Sequined with difference. At the moment of enlightenment, when the Buddha touched his finger to the ground, all the leaves fell off the Bodhi tree. Religion

has the touch of a bird through grass. Wood duck, gadwall, northern pintail. On the day Robert Creeley died the Dow closed up 10540. The Dow closed down 1130 on the day Prince released *Purple Rain*.

You call a yellow leaf gold to stop a child's crying. Golden rain tree, rusty backhaw, sycamore, elm. A penmanship branches across sky, stiff as dialect, hard as the 14th amendment.

An eddy in a river makes a small cup of world. Hooded merganser, cooper's hawk, northern harrier. Write your headnote in the sky, like the court reporter, J. C. Bancroft Davis who wrote, *obiter dictum*, corporations have the same rights as individuals. It is sad

to be among people who don't read, who fear art because they think it mocks them. The river is nothing but river. Or your mother. Or the nation. Merck, Microsoft, Pfizer. Draw water, carry firewood, bear this instant. In the prolonged present, you hear dollars tick. Leaves static. Leaves distract. On the day Robert Rauschenberg died the Dow closed up 12828. Water rushes over stones with a touch as light as a court stenographer. Winter branches scribble

obiter dictum. Nothing changes from generation to generation except the thing seen. Rusty backhaw, golden rain tree, 3M, Alcoa, AT&T. Hot linked and jumpy as the sunset over a gas station

and that makes composition, makes an index, makes a footpath out of yellow leaves.

June 14—The Dow Closes Down 10192

The names of 62 birds are listed in dry erase marker
what we do and see exceeds conceptual categories

what counts as real depends upon the dry erase board
joins in a continuous loop with information technology

sympathy as feedback/dialogue
sympathy in the comment box

yellow bird (unnamed) at the feeder (likes this)
a squirrel eats pears from the tree

bluegreen dragonflies fly by the tomatoes
release

the long lag between
thought|sentence

what at first seems like a Graph Theory problem
is a simple Longest Common Subsequence problem

just as yesterday's seminary students with thick library books
suggest an unwillingness to invest in certain claims

to the bird I seem bigger than I am
to the sky—another matter all together (3 people like this)

Susan Briante

Note about the poems included:

These poems form part of a lyric response to the economic crisis of 2008. "The Market as Composition" takes the line "Nothing changes from generation to generation except the thing seen" from Gertrude Stein's "Composition as Explanation" and uses data retrieved from on-line stock market index archives. In "June 14—The Dow Closes Down 10192," the lines "at first seems like a Graph Theory problem/ is a simple Longest Common Subsequence problem" comes from entry UVa 10192 on the www.algorithmist.com wiki.

Stephen Burt
Manifest Stephanie

Manifesto: a program; an emphatic set of directions, especially in art or politics; a document meant to found a movement or to produce followers and imitators; a call to arms; a claim to collective authority based in part (as the scholar Martin Puchner has noticed—his example is the Communist Manifesto) on events that have yet to occur.

Manifest (noun): a list of goods expected or loaded on a commercial transport, to be checked against whatever arrives.

Manifest (verb): to appear; to become material; to come into material existence (e.g. as an avatar of a god or demon) at a particular place and time.

Manifest (adjective): overt, apparent, concrete, confirmed by the evidence of the senses, no longer open to reasonable doubt, *as against* covert, hermetic, secret, implicit, requiring interpretation, still unknown.

Note that a manifesto does not change—it says, or appears to say, the same thing every time (though like all texts it can undergo new editions). A manifest, though, has to be altered, with signatures, each time some cargo is added or taken away, and a god, a hero or a demon— in the relevant religious systems, myths, stories and tabletop roleplaying games—can manifest as a new avatar each time.

I don't want to write a manifesto: the meaning and history of "manifesto" now seem alien to me, and to the poems I want to write, though not to all the poems I want to read. Instead, I want to write a manifest;

to manifest myself; to make a list; to make clear certain hypotheses about the purpose of poetry, about why some of us keep writing and reading it, even or especially when we are still trying to figure out what it can do.

*

"One of the favorite maxims of my father [the physicist Niels Bohr] was the distinction between the two sorts of truths—profound truths recognized by the fact that the opposite is also a profound truth, in contrast to trivialities" (Hans Bohr).

"[Theoretical physicist Wolfgang Pauli] broke equipment in every lab he went to. But as his fame grew, and as he entered more labs, the lab workers noticed that he didn't even have to touch a piece of equipment. Whenever he visited the lab, things would stop working spontaneously. It happened again and again. It got bad enough that some of his friends . . . wouldn't allow him in their labs anymore. . . . Supposedly, the more important the theorist, the more equipment breaks down around them" (Esther Inglis-Arkell).

*

Panels in comics—so writes the comics artist and theorist Scott McCloud—can be "image-specific," if the image tells the story, or "word-specific," if the words tell the story, or "parallel" if words and pictures tell different stories, or "interdependent" if we need to look at them both to figure out what's going on. All these ways to make a comics panel have their place, and long-form comics may use all of them. What talented comics artists tend to avoid—though you see them a lot in old superhero books—is the "duo-specific" panel, where the speech balloons and/or the captions tell you just what you already see.

*

Advice widely attributed to Coco Chanel (though she may never have said it): after you get dressed, before you leave the house, look in the mirror and take one thing off. It is advice you can take only if you already wear jewelry, or other accessories, unnecessary things; and it is good advice, especially in poems.

*

"Manifestos tend to present themselves as mere means to an end,
demanding to be judged not by their rhetorical or literary merits—their
poetry—but by their ability to change the world. Marx, however, helps
us understand that it is their form, not their particular complaints
and demands, that articulates most succinctly the desires and hopes,
maneuvers and strategies of modernity: to create points of no return;
to make history; to fashion the future" (Martin Puchner).

What poet would not want to help fashion the future? But only some
want a divorce from history; only some want points of no return.

*

"Manifest destiny," the now infamous phrase, seems to have been
coined by the newspaper editor John J. O'Sullivan (a friend of the
young Walter Whitman) in 1845: he meant that the United States of
America was clearly already expanding to the West, that resistance was
futile, and that American citizens ought to help that (as it turned out,
genocidal) process along.

There is a version of poetry which says that it ought to address what
is *not* manifest, what cannot be made manifest, what is not destined,
but rather tenuous, imaginary, hard or impossible for us to see clearly,
or impossible to see (since it is abstract: the soul, or the personality,
or the imagination, or that which lacks exchange value) at all.

The poem has no destiny that can be known in advance. Or, if you
prefer, that *is* the poem's destiny: to make manifest what cannot be
known in advance; to manifest in language what, before this poem,
language could not show. (The poet and theorist Allen Grossman left
this Earth while I was compiling this manifest; I suspect that this
paragraph, in particular, imitates or even paraphrases him.)

*

Stories about revolutions, about subversions, about the fall of an
unjust regime, are (relatively) easy to tell: they are stories about the
fulfillment of individuals, who team up to overthrow what already
IS—and (Alexander Pope, and God, notwithstanding) whatever IS has
problems enough.

Stories about what happens next—about the day after the day after the revolution—are harder to tell, and much harder to make popular: they involve compromises, and sacrifices, not just in practice but in principle, and they can end in ways that leave many people better off, but no one goal fulfilled.

Any theory of poetry to which I would subscribe has to leave room not just for revolutions in poetic language and taste, for originality as "revolution," but also for one year after the revolution, for the weird sadness and the exhausting compromise of trying to help new things become manifest, trying to let them get built.

*

The opposite of the manifesto (a collective document both predicting, and prescribing, future action) might be the autobiography (a document by a single individual that describes and explains her past). But the opposite of autobiography might also be the lyric poem: a place made of words that can seem to exist outside time, where "you yourself were never quite yourself/ And did not want nor have to be" (Wallace Stevens).

Does that make the lyric poem the opposite, or the ghostly double, or the body double, of the manifesto? When does a lyric poem tell you what to do?

*

"Poetry" "makes" "nothing" "happen." "It" "survives."

*

I should like to dissociate myself (but I can never dissociate myself completely) from the history of men telling men and women what to do.

"Only [with the manifesto] did the avant-garde have available the proper instrument to articulate its state of being advanced, its break with the past and affinity to the future, and only then did it speak succinctly and aggressively with a single collective voice." (Martin Puchner) To which compare Rimbaud: *Je est un autre.*

*

It is a part of my very essence, an indispensable part of being me, that I announce, quite accurately, from time to time, that I am somebody else.

It's tempting for me to make such claims all about gender (since I am usually Stephen, and sometimes Stephanie, in day-to-day life and in poems): but that would be both false to other trans people's experience (many trans people have one gender, all the time—it's just not the one they were assigned at birth) and false to a few more general claims about poetry, of which gender is just an example (OK, a really big example, but still). Here are the claims:

In poetry you have to be yourself in one way, but not in others. If you do it right you can choose which way, and which others.

You do not always have to make the same choice, or a consistent choice, from poem to poem—though maybe you do, within a given poem: that depends on the kind of poem.

Poetry is a mode of becoming, more often and more effectively than it is, or has been, a mode of being.

No one should *consistently* tell poets who to be, or where to go, or what to become, or how to manifest ourselves.

*

Write for one reader who is *just like* you—if you do not write for someone who knows everything you know, you will not make your own poems.

Write also for a reader who is *not much like you*—if you do not write for that reader you will not be able to know how and whether your poem can stand, apart from the person who wrote it: you won't know whether it *represents* (rather than being, simply, a thing made by) you.

The only person who is exactly like you, who gets all your references and understands all your goals (before you can make them manifest) is you.

*

If you can't let yourself write things you don't believe, or try saying things you would not support, then you will never know what you believe.

If you trust yourself—or anyone else—consistently and completely, you'll never improve. (By "you" I mean "me.")

If you can't trust yourself, you will never trust anyone else. (By "you" I mean "me.")

*

A manifesto assumes, if not always a collective voice, a collective audience: people who might take coordinated or homogenous action, based on these words. Poetry, on the other hand...

1978 Stephanie

I

I made myself. Mommy and Daddy were proud, in that order.
I didn't mail myself like a letter some other kids
already knew. I learned to use stamps. They stuck to my thumb
without any glue. I didn't have any permission.

2

There was a snowstorm that lasted three days
and a cavern of monochrome memory. There were board games, and
    a pencil-and-paper game
where the object was to figure out the object of the game.
There was a stack of broad-rule writing paper, and a stapled
    calendar,
and a 64-pack of sparkly rainbow crayons, to make each week look
    different
since they all started out black and white, and all the same.

3

O grapefruit (as color and flavor). O never quite rightly tied laces. O
    look,
up there on the uneven climbing bars,
too hot to touch where the sun touches them.
O think of the lost Chuck Taylors. The lost Mary Janes.

Stephen Burt

A Nickel on Top of a Penny

I am going to disappear in Belmont,
after taking a walk in intermittent rain.
I will vanish one day in Belmont—don't correct me—
on a warm day like today, a Thursday, in fall.

I know it even more than I know how we all want
contradictory things, like security and excitement,
immortality, hang gliders, gumdrops, a home, and all
the space in the world—Eden, Paris, Tokyo, Cockaigne.

My writing hand hurts. To the good friends who asked me to dinner,
I'm afraid I should tell you not to expect me.
When you set the table, say, "Stephanie couldn't be here,
although we were good to her; we gave her presents

for Christmas and such; we answered most of her letters,
importunate as they became; we tried not to offend her;
we sat through her chatter about piano lessons,

and telephoned her in the midst of a snowstorm last year.
We think we could not have treated her any better.
We never believed she'd simply disappear."

after Cesar Vallejo

Jen Campbell
Manifesto

When I pick up a pen I hear the *once upon a times*. I hear the voices of
many different women. I try to find my voice amongst all of theirs.
I am in awe of them.

Because once upon a time there was a woman.

She mothered the world. She cut off her breast to be a better warrior.
She was an off-the-page disciple. She built an ark in her spare time.
She signed it *anon* with the branch of a tree.

She ate an apple, once. She heard it was good for her soul.

She merged with the creatures and learnt how to sing.
Men saw her and were shipwrecked.
She smiled and slid back under the water.

She slept in the underworld and the world turned cold.

She grew her hair to the floor.
She threw her hair out the window.
She cut off all her hair.

She could not love. She could not write poetry.
She was Viola and she was dressed up as a boy.

She was a witch. She was burned at the stake.

She was Little Red Riding Hood. She had sex with the wrong man. He was dressed as a wolf. He swallowed her whole. She curled up in his stomach until another man cut her out.

She was Little Red Riding Hood. She was forced down the wrong path. The man was dressed as a wolf. He tried to swallow her whole. She skinned the wolf and wore his fur. All the men ran away.

She was the wolf.
If she were a book then she would be banned.

She threw herself in front of a horse.

She drew vaginas as flowers. She *was* a flower.
She was a rose. She was a huge Venus flytrap.

She slept with women. She slept with men. She was a whore and a slut.
Legitimate rape and easy rape.
She listened to middle-aged men discussing abortion on the radio.

She bit her broken nails. She stamped her broken feet.

She wore a balaclava and sang in a church.
She was on fire. She was a fire.
She was all eyes, and all mouth, and all soul.

At the weekend, she went out and planted a whole row of bloody apple trees. Then she planted herself, and waited to grow.

*

Once upon a time there was *this* woman.
And she listened and she saw.
And then she wrote. She wrote. She wrote.

etymology

In the garden we are surrounded by lady bugs.
Birds, Caitlin whispers. Her electric hair flying. We feel
for leaf bones. Pound our faces into liquorice soil.
No one is home and the old house is sinking. Next
door there is a man who crouches below hedges.
He watches. Through the petals
we are orange girls. Caitlin peeling her hair like fruit rind.
Some days I feel she is a hotel. She needs cleaning
from all the ghosts that continue to sleep inside of her.
She has a grass stain on her upper lip. Pickling.
These spiders are whales on stilts, she laughs.

Jen Campbell

the exorcism of the north sea

On Sundays we sing.
Ghost birds. You lead us
to the southern cliffs
with our Girl Guide tents.
The sun is ours.
We have verses to prove it
tucked in the hems of our
mid-winter pockets.
We are snow globes.
Along the rows of
white-washed caravans
young boys peer
out and whistle if
their mums aren't home.
Everything is seen through
murky glass. The sea lurches.
Someone should save
the soul of her. Lukewarm
and watered down.
Holding all the girls
in bathing suits.
We stretch out our
carol sheets
and hum like bees.

Kara Candito
Destroy Yourself!
Some Notes on the Poetics of Travel

*

To travel is to understand the self as multiple and acted upon by the contingencies of place. How else do I make sense of my two childhood selves? The American only child who dreaded spending summers with her father's large family in a tiny village in southern Italy and the Italian-American who cried upon returning to the quiet television and linoleum universe of her Massachusetts life. In Italy, my father, the stoic suit and tie atheist, kissed men on both cheeks and took Communion like he meant it. In Italy, I was the American cousin with a funny accent. In Massachusetts, I was the Italian girl with the big family who missed birthday parties for her cousins' baptisms.

Tarfia Faizullah's speaker addresses this contradictory plurality in "En Route to Bangladesh, Another Crisis of Faith," a poem from her first collection, *Seam* (2014):

> I take my place among
> this damp horde of men
> and women who look like me—
> because I look like them—
> because I am ashamed
> of their bodies that reek so
> unabashedly of body—
> because I can—because I am
> an American . . .

The poet identifies and abjects. She is jet-lagged and porous, both self and other.

*

"Should we have stayed at home and thought of here?" asks Bishop's speaker in "Questions of Travel." To is to say *yes, please* to restlessness and homesickness, to an acknowledgement of the abyss between imagination and lived experience. I do my research. I construct my mythology of said city or country with full knowledge that it will be dismantled and reconstituted by reality. The poet is a perpetual traveler. She courts a self-annihilating drive between identity and nonidentity, and knowing and unknowing

*

In another life, I marketed Frommer's travel guides for a publishing company in Hoboken, N.J. Every morning, I'd bike across East 9th St., from Alphabet City to the Christopher St. PATH station, dodging cab doors and wayward pedestrians. On the train, I'd dread the cropped, glossy jacket images plastered all over my paltry cubicle: a Medieval castle on a hill (France); cerulean blue domed rooftops (Greece); a charro slouching on his horse (Mexico); long-tail boats moored in emerald water (Thailand).

Like manifestos, travel guides are in the business of surface knowing. Glutted with superlatives and promises of *insider knowledge*, they crop the landscape into stylized coherence. They're the unsolicited advice men in suits offer foreign women on trains. Don't drink the water. Avoid this neighborhood. Watch out for your handbag at this market. Go here for the best fruit, here for the best coffee. Don't stay at this hotel, the owners are thieves. I can't and don't want to instruct because I write as I travel; to be dismantled and re-contextualized.

*

In the U.S., I'm short and olive-skinned. In Mexico, I'm a tallish güera. In Wuhan, China, where I've spent the last three winters teaching "An Introduction to English Literature for TESOL Graduate Students," I'm a towering pre-verbal child. When I lose my local guide on the bus, I gesture furiously at a kind stranger and flash a card with an address written in characters I don't understand. How do I reinvent the world in the absence of familiar language? How do I find my way home?

*

The first lines of a poem appear like a new country through a plane window. The topography falls into place: significant monuments; the alignment of rivers, roads and mountains. Its modes of discovery will be easy: enter, eat and snap some pictures.

Of course, nothing goes as planned. There are missed trains, blisters, lost phone chargers and the inconstant hours of restaurants recommended on Trip Advisor. There are odd cravings for the comforting language of turkey sandwiches and reliable plumbing.

*

Like the poems I want to read and write, travel blurs the borders between domestic and exotic. Last winter, alone and sick in Wuhan, China, I found myself on a park bench listening to the singing of school children in baggy sport uniforms. Maybe it was the dead smell of fish rolling in off East Lake, or the clouded, particular light that approximated spring in New England, but suddenly the lyrics of a song from third grade music class returned: *The Nina, the Pinta, the Santa Maria, sail them over the sea.* How terribly sentimental and imperialistic they sounded to my adult self. How strangely urgent they felt at that feverish moment on the other side of the world. Once, I kept a dime in the zip-pocket of my pink high-tops for calling home if I got lost or otherwise dispossessed. In Wuhan, I unlocked my iPhone. The screen read *1:45 p.m., December 31, 2013.* In the left-hand corner where the service bars belonged, it said *No Service.*

Works Cited

Bishop, Elizabeth. "Questions of Travel." *The Complete Poems: 1927–1979.* Farrar Straus and Giroux, 1983, pp. 93–94.

Faizullah, Tarfia. "En Route to Bangladesh, Another Crisis of Faith." *Seam.* Southern Illinois UP, 2014, p. 64.

Kara Candito

Egypt Journal: The Poet's Condition

When the evening wind starts to blow south from Asia
        and on the radio, Um Kulthoum, the Egyptian
Billie Holiday, aches out a song about the callused thumbs
            of memory, about being a barefoot girl from the Delta;
when the man I love twists the ice tray twice, and drops

three cubes into my hibiscus, I remember the ménage a trois
            I wanted but talked myself out of one hazy night
in college and leaving him at the table with Turkish coffee
            and cardamom seeds, I walk bare-sleeved where
the guidebook says DANGER and the street is a garish

human theatre, the bazaar a winepress of cheap consolation
            prizes—stuffed plastic camels and bright, slippery
beads that say why wonder at this time of night how
            the belly dancers slam their finger cymbals so hard,
yet habitually, why their skin burns, so perfectly flawed

like the cracks in the pyramids in morning sun, how they
            paint their eyes that high, sexual black that makes
the fundamentalists, who are tugging their beards somewhere,
            rabid to stop this dance that celebrates simply
the body's light, which is the din of a hundred conversations

in a small room, as if all of Gezira swallowed a radio,
            as if the Nile parted like legs of phosphorescent
light that I follow into the center of the center of the city,
            as in storm, where everything is still as the wall
Saladin built around the Citadel, a place of clean lines

and the crusaders' captured sighs, where he could rest
      and where I stop tonight to search for my face,
or anything familiar in the sky, in the dirty moon,
      I am thinking, *How small I am,*
I am thinking, *I will write this down.*

Kara Candito

V's Dream on the Plane from Mexico City to Chicago

It began with aduanas
and my mother's childhood name;
escalators, drug-sniffing dogs;
      you, the night wind cloaking Insurgentes
and riding a stolen a bike past the blackened
      monuments of national heroes. I was following

Porfirio Diaz, but maybe he wasn't
Porfirio Diaz. It began in a public bathroom
with a dripping faucet where my mother
      and I hunched like animals in front of the urinals.
In the middle, a florescent lamp, tarmac, a torn
      tablecloth. The light moved

like a virus. In the middle, my mother
spat and rubbed her palms together—
an undersong of saliva and gardenia
      and *mijo never, never marry a gringa.*
In the middle, we crouched in the front
      of the urinals as if already

it were winter and we'd never stand
together again. Outside, snakes curled
beneath the nogal trees where
      the swallows were falling.
A tearing sound,

like two possible endings—
me voy, me voy,
con permiso. Now,
      something flies away,
or something is poisoned.

Bruce Cohen
Poetry Manifesto

My poetry manifesto changes almost momentarily. What I believe, slurping my alphabet soup, will most likely not be true after my catnap. The seductive blank page: nothing exists till I am involved! As John Clare said: "The place we occupy seems all the world." My favorite poet, Weldon Kees, said it another way: "Rugs, vases, panatelas in a humidor. They would fill the room if Robinson came in." But who is this Robinson character, this alienated, fragile, anti-heroic, everyman alter ego? We all must have one. But at this very moment, I am thinking about the wonderful Polish poet, Wisława Szymborska, and her famous lines: "I prefer the absurdity of writing poems to the absurdity of not writing poems." The obvious implication is that the world, whether we're living in it or making art from it, or dreaming about it, is absurd. The equation is as follows: Life or Art are the only choices, both of which, perhaps, are bipolar and cannot be conducted simultaneously = absurdity. And, as Louise Glück acknowledges in her wonderful essay about being a poet: "The fundamental experience of the writer is helplessness." Yes, what brings me to try to compose poems is that feeling of hopeful hopelessness and wonder and how the world feels complex and illusive and allusive and mysterious and absurd and I would say surreal but what is more surreal than the world as it is? Did you know that Walt Disney, a whack job himself, who built esoteric tunnels under Disneyland to spy on his guests, enlisted Salvador Dali to draw the cartoons to the original version of *Fantasia*. The idea was nixed as the "public" was not, at that point, ready for Dali and his madness and his waxed mustache. A little too edgy is what I like, a little too ahead of TIME. However, as Rilke said: "Most of my life has been spent not understanding..." I, too, lollygag in my own stupidity and I find myself oblivious to a good portion of the external world. Am I delusional enough to think the act of writing poems makes me understand the subtle nuances and complexities of life better? Yup. After all, all I want is to be entertained and stimulated and feel world-included and be left alone and be a little less pathetic and somehow more empowered by having people love me. Am I arrogant to say I love anyone worthy of my love? Ah, egocentric standards! I am attracted to language that makes me envision the world in a way that is a departure from my expected "reality". I like using the wrong words on purpose or mistake. Also, word order is a choice! (Think Berryman). Andre Breton argued that we are under the reign of terror of logic, but there are other types of logic, logics I grasp on intuitive and instinctual levels that I can't quite articulate. Think how goofy you sound when trying to recite the narrative of a dream you had to someone over breakfast. At some point, you stare at a glazed expression and say, "never mind." But we are connected, maybe through our universal uncertainty. Susan Mitchell says: "When I am certain that I have nothing in common with a person, I tell myself that we both know what water tastes like, and neither of us can describe that taste." That's the bond I have with poems I love. I have no desire to explain them away. And maybe I couldn't even if I wanted to: how does one describe our choices in love? Doesn't The Rush arrive before language? Think about how newborn babies love their mothers when they recognize their smell in the dark. I am always trying to write a poem better than I can write a poem. When I mentioned to my wife that I was going upstairs to try to compose my manifesto she said I must have too much time on my hands and that people who write manifestos should not mention manifestos to people who don't have one. Maybe I should zip my trap: "The first rule of Fight Club is to never speak of Fight Club." But I would like to say a few things. Poetry is the linguistic vehicle by which I arrive at those almost impossible to grasp fleeting notions, emotions, psychological dilemmas, and vacancies of the heart. There is so much my intellect cannot solve and I am constantly in a state of curious awe and dumbfounded amusement. Poetry is sly, always making finer and finer paradoxical distinctions between the secrets we keep and the secrets we don't share. As Dean Young emphatically states in *The Art of Recklessness*: "Some impurities can make water clearer."

Works Cited

Clare, John. "November." *Northborough Sonnets*, edited by Eric Robinson, David Powell, and P. M. S. Dawson, Midnag and Carcanet, 1995, p. 67.

Glück, Louise. *Proofs and Theories: Essays on Poetry*. Ecco, 1994.

Kees, Weldon. "Robinson." *The Collected Poems of Weldon Kees*, edited by Donald Justice, Alfred A. Knopf, 2004.

Mitchell, Susan. *The Poet's Notebook: Excerpts from the Notebooks of Contemporary American Poets*, edited by Stephen Kuusisto, Deborah Tall, and David Weiss, W. W. Norton, 1995, p. 202.

Rilke, Maria Rainer. *The Notebooks of Malte Laurids Brigge*. Penguin Classics, 2009.

Szymborska, Wisława. "Possibilities." *Poems: New and Collected*. Mariner Books, 2000.

Young, Dean. *The Art of Recklessness: Poetry as Assertive Force and Contradiction*. Graywolf Press, 2010.

Bruce Cohen

Follain Combs the Parking Lot for His Vehicle after the Movie

When the lost couple stops to ask directions I feel obligated to inquire how it is they can see me. An imaginary girl lives behind where I live. She wanders over when I'm futzing in my garden, hoeing hills for purple Peruvian potatoes. Ominously overhanging the garden shed, (ipso facto imaginary) there was a diseased elm, leafless, bark-less, for a decade. Likewise the girl doesn't ever wear her coat, even in winter, but the snow finds a way to avoid her. Just yesterday it finally fell, but not satisfyingly, (no one shouted timber with an exaggerated euphonious second syllable) as the fall was suspended by the Y of a living oak. My neighbor girl said the elm's half-falling seemed decaffeinated. *You know, it's like when my mother brews coffee in the afternoon. She slides her secret bottle from her apron & pours a small correction into her mug.*

It's wonderful how lies & deceptive gestures repeated enough become true. There's one disturbing memory everyone can't shake or talk about that has no redeeming context with any other part of her life. To teach myself patience I chop down trees just to watch them grow back. I deconstruct well-constructed theories on the fallibility of pre-cut items. I *hear* trees, my tree cracking under its own weight, so begin my diatribe on freefalling as chloroform vacates leaves, leaving behind exquisite autistic autumn colors. American children, when asked to draw a tree, begin with the trunk. Aboriginal children draw a circle because that's the hawks' view, the way this couple leaving the movies have their own lingo-code & set of eyes.

They forgot where they parked; I saw them circling the dark lot pressing buttons on their key rings in a kind of mild panic. There are so many types of light: the departing rows of headlights, flickering streetlights, the hollow glow of a man's face lighting his cigarette, the brightness faltering within us & so many wear sunglasses indoors at night. Sometimes evening clouds appear as black organic flour poured over ghosts.

The imaginary girl confessed she practiced kissing no one in the basement while she picked at her scabs, ripped out strands of hair, & was startled when she heard her mother trip down the stairs. She believes kisses should remain intentional. Nothing ought to be automatic. I asked how it is she can see me. She echoed & we chuckled. There is non-verbal talk within talk. Infinite & indefinite trees falling. There are forests of gestures & glances, half-moons & half-finished sentences. Disjointed, disparate utterances we understand perfectly. Of course there is that which is too painful to say & trees falling & anxious buttons, a panicky squeezing of buttons & a more frenetic unbuttoning of buttons & more trees than anyone can count & the tranquility of a tree splintered in a windstorm & people falling down stairs & trees half-falling.

Sometimes I go days without changing the burned out light bulb till darkness surrenders its sense of urgency. I know every night is on the brink of an anniversary, as the drunk, at dawn, thinks this drink will be his last. People hardly even exist. Behind where we live. And for such a short time. In such distracted boarded up tree forts, where each nail is quite intentional. I am fidgety like a perpetual insomniac who paces the corridors reciting out loud the dark Braille of walls, worrying where the staircase begins.

The Uncanny

Suppose a rational man
Rations himself into an irrational man.
Construct his lifelike manikin.
Take a snapshot of this semi-rational
Manikin. Paint an impressionistic
Portrait of the snapshot—speckles galore,
Then take a digital photo of the painting
& send it viral. With a fishing knife,
Kill the man. With a sledgehammer,
Crush the manikin: take a match to the original
Photograph (sepia). Gash the painting
With the bloody fishing knife.
The math, primarily subtraction, is subtext.
Imagine squirt gunning acid on a handsome face.
You are left with the disfigurement, immortality
Of the man & his final image has a life
Of its own but has evolved into art. Notice
A homeless man sleeping over a sewer grate
In a cobalt sub-zero sleeping bag, his head
Covered—his entire body zipped in.
You see the shape of his human form
& can only assume it is a man.
It could be a woman & maybe it is not
Even a person. You wonder if the man is
Not sleeping but dead: overdose or overexposure?
You come to *realize* which is different
From discovery—the sleeping bag is not a sleeping
Bag but a sculptured bronze painted speckled-blue
With a human-shaped-bulge apparently
Sleeping inside a sleeping bag. The title:

This is Not A Man Sleeping Inside a Sleeping Bag.
You are curious about the mosquito on the wall.
Is it part of the exhibit?
If you stare long enough
You can detect it is not an actual mosquito.
You think you hear a symphony of buzzing.
A continuous film of nothing
But raindrops on gray pavement
Is ten thousand black & white still photographs
Of eggs frying in butter,
The elevator is miniature (five inches high)
& the female watchman
(This is her part-time gig; she's a Community
College student) says wouldn't it be
Awesome if we could fit inside.
Which miniature world would it take us to?
Ten thousand Chinese children hand paint
Pebbles to resemble sunflower seeds.
They will require reading glasses before their time.
A man dumps ten thousand imitation seeds
On the museum floor & on his hands
& knees selects the most pristine,
Only a tight fistful, & places them in an hermetically
Sealed hand blown glass jar. His knees ache
In that way knees hurt when you crawl
Over pebbles. Turquoise toilets & sinks,
Avocado kitchen appliances from the 1970's
With matching wallpaper & rotary wall phones.
The phone never rings but as soon as you
Step outside the phone rings.
Is it your presence or a manikin that has not been smashed?
Is it me or *is it just me* you ask.
Do all people actually die?
Is the mosquito transporting your hemoglobin in his belly,
Part of your life to another country?

Bruce Cohen

The man sleeping in his sleeping
Bag doesn't seem to stir but sleeping
People often don't unless
They are involved in a nightmare.
Are you engaged in a nightmare?
Of course there are microscopic
Elevators in our minds that don't stop
On every floor. Of course as much
As we don't label them 13th floors exist.
Wouldn't it be awesome if we could
Get off to defy our perception of the unlucky?
I am chipmunk-stuffing this abundance
Of sunflower seeds & spitting the shells.
I'm outside so it's okay.
I'm inside & nobody is watching so it's
Okay. Molar cracking. They are
Infinitely salty & I have convinced myself
I am not thirsty, floating 32 days on a life raft,
32 days, a life raft deflating so slowly
I don't notice the air escaping,
After my plane has been shot down.
There is a real fishing knife
& real fish skeletons & candy seagulls.

Erica Dawson
Confessional Activism

I'm a black woman. I live in the United States. I have a Shih-Tzu. I suffer from mental illness. I'm a professor and a poet. My world shapes me; I shape it back.

I prize poems of social activism explicitly demanding a need for change: poems like Langston Hughes' "Let America Be America Again." We need poems like this, so necessary in a world crippled by tragedy, crime, and hate. I'm honored when people say I, too, sing America. And while I know that I'm no Langston Hughes, I'm moved enough by our society's sickness to call it out on paper, as he did. Minutes after a jury found George Zimmerman not guilty for the death of Trayvon Martin, I started a cento comprised of rap lyrics. When someone didn't like my slang in a different poem, I pulled up Urbandictionary.com and looked for even more slang to use next time. The world often leaves me feeling defeated—damned, even. I want to give our tragedies a voice, my voice, offering readers the chance to engage with and question our culture. That is the responsibility of any artist.

It is also our responsibility to give the most personal tragedies a voice, so I equally prize poems explicitly about the self, poems we call Confessional. I'm not Plath, Sexton, or Lowell any more than I'm Langston Hughes; but I do write poems about mental illness as much as I write about race, publicly disclosing my struggles with symptoms, treatment, and hope.

It's to everyone's misfortune that poems like these often shoulder the same stigma as mental illness in general. I give our society credit for its growing attention to those who suffer from it, but there's still the lingering subtext of "Suck it up and move on; get some meds and get over yourself." Confessional work, for many critics, translates to "navel-gazing," an overblown sense of self-importance—selfishness.

To the critics, I say confessional poetry is not some self-indulgent purge of emotions. I write poems about myself in an effort to understand those emotions, to give myself permission to experience them and not rid myself of them, to learn from them, and to give others the chance to think about their world in the same way. If this isn't socially-relevant, I'm not sure what is.

The relationship between writer and audience, no matter how small that audience is, especially in a time where we ask ourselves if poetry even matters, puts every poem, no matter how personal to the poet's mind and body, in conversation with the body politic.

Any activism begins with "I": the individual's mind and the most solitary activity: thinking. Hughes was adamant about the relationship of his personal life to the life of all black people. In the same vein, I believe my experiences are both singular and plural: pertaining to many, whether it's black people, women, heterosexuals in their thirties, people swallowing several psychotropic drugs a day to stay alive—whomever. I write from the truths and realities of my thoughts based on my perceptions. This is why I create and recreate, iamb after iamb. The poet is open and vulnerable, the space of a poem like a serein: rain falling after sunset from a sky with no visible clouds. There's nothing to hide behind, and there's no need for shelter. Expressing that openness is the poet's power, no matter the subject, no matter the pronoun: never barred, always exposed.

Ideation X

(I)

I'd give a fuck about the world outside
If Tennessee and its American
Holly swallowed me whole;

(II)

if Thuja Green
Giants would grow to armies, thick in toothed
Stinging nettle;

(III)

if banjoes reigned, string plucked
By plectrum;

(IV)

if the sky at Greens' View seethed
Nashville and boiled over;

(V)

if green plains
Curled with the breeze that wreathed white Skullcap grins.

(VI)

I'd give an arm for rye at 2 a.m.

(VII)

I'd give a leg to have my pulse slow down,
An eye to keep from crying, give this machine
Connected to my butterfly-pricked vein
If I could go back to my summer home
Where I won't dial 911 or hear
The plan to ship me down to Vanderbilt.

(VIII)

                                    What if
My voice, all swoll' up in the chest, and broad,
Had said, *that box cutter you found was just
For packages;* said, *I agree; there will
Be someone else; It's August; nine times three
Is twenty-seven; yes, ma'am: no, there ain't
No misery that's worth nobody's life.*

(IX)

I wouldn't say I have a knife at home,
Nor would I swear I've often heard the cows
In Tennessee declare, *no more of your
Imaginings.* In Cincinnati streets,
I saw a brown calf chew on too-big cud.
I lifted up his ear to see the pink.
In Tampa, I am out for blood.

(X)

                                                        If I
Could only find the means to watch the world
Implode—its red hot core naked, salt-thick
With blues—and, then, recuperate as if,
Like all of us, it has something to prove.

Erica Dawson

Florida Officers tied to KKK

I live just 85 miles away.
A *city nigger*. They've got pillow cases
Over their heads for makeshift hoods—a day
Of reckoning, initiations, traces,

Inside a house, of nearby citrus groves.
I'd like to make the trip to Fruitland Park,
Rap on the door and tell them how, in droves,
We're coming and we're big and black and bark

Like the animals they say we are. But in
Reality, it's me. This is a poem.
And is that tolerance? A fly will buzz
Around a rind like it's its only home.
Rinds have evolved with a much thicker skin.
What is necessity if not because

Of something? What is if then then or now
What now if not self-reparation done
For some survival—just a swooning bow
Taken in thanks the worst is over? Run

Is what I wish I'd think, until I've found
The state's southernmost point and let my feet
Drown in the waves waking my knees. I'd meet
My harnessed blame: I did not stand my ground.

It's easier to call my faults, say all
Those officers don't know no better, nor
Do I; say Erica, you're small in tall
Vast grapefruit trees, and slighter than a spoor
Of gator wakes in rivers. Still, I sprawl
When dreaming of the pith and underscore.

Sean Thomas Dougherty
In the Absence of Others I Wanted Something Brave

Yes, I accept I declare to no one. I get on the open road. I remember my father drinking. I'll forget my name except for the ache of my bones. I knew this much was mine. For the poem can call me sweetcakes. Tell me we are out of vegetables. Kiss me full on the mouth. These taboos we try to explain. The data proves it is difficult. Go to the diner: order your sausage and eggs, sup on the slit throats of swine.

Blood red leaves like knives cut the air of autumn.

Call up the critics, the professors with their funny hats. Ask them what they know about suffering? Their long litanies and references will make the most colicky child fall fast asleep.

What lullaby but the winter wind off the lake, and needing a new coat.

A poem is a wing, a bird without wings. A poem is a sparrow that walks across my snowy lawn this winter, when the wind chill is near 15 below, a poem is a kind of absent song.

A poem is not a bullet, though some may claim. But I imagine a poem could be a bullet. Or is the poem the hole that is left when the bullet goes through? A poem is a kind of absent song.

A poem is not a carburetor. Or a poem could be the carburetor of the human heart. A carburetor that has not been cleaned, a carburetor full of gunk. But I suspect the poem is really written in the scratches in the piston. I suspect the poem is really the gasoline. A poem is a burning pool of gasoline.

Sometimes I read these things that say a poem is a theory, or driven by a theory, or written by a certain theory. I see those kinds of poems all the time, some of them I actually *feel,* they have some *body,* some of them climb the ladders of the stair. But is that what a poem is, that makes a poem what we are? The writer bending over to type her theory poem, the hands of another writing his theory poem. All the collisions of Empire and class?

I am eating violets. I am pissing on a parked police car outside the Day Old Donuts shop. See *Endowed* (I mean how funny, how masculine, how drearily obscene). And I imagine the cold wind outside clattering against their tenured walls. They've named their house. The one in Oberlin. They have an Edwardian garden while they declaim they are the Avant Garde! Viva the Revolution! *As long as my hands remain clean.* Collaborators with a dead regime.

A poem is not a theory. You don't want me to say this but the poem is a cunt, sewn shut. Every stitch is the poem. A poem is a shackled wrist. It is a hundred Pakistani girls with their throats slit. It is Selma. It is Ferguson. It is *nigger* scrawled in an East Side bar's bathroom stall. Is this too direct? Sometimes the elusive is witness. I have written that before. Sometimes the only witness is a brick.

Put down your pen I want to say. Drive out to the edge of town to the State Prison. A poem is the theory of a prisoner. Or the prisoners, bending their backs in their orange jumpsuits, slave labor on the road works. This is where I live. We live in a time where every theory is a failure. We have no need for more literary theories. When cops kill us and the government has slave detention camps up and down the border, and men in dark suits like white hoods make profits.

The poem is not happy. The poem looks at the theory and spits. The poem takes your identity and says, you have forgotten your skin. Put your fingers inside yourself and taste yourself. Peel back your foreskin. Take your theories and your clean hands and go fuck yourself, the poem says. A poem is a *fuck you* to your theory.

The poem does not need an award. *The poem is for those who've lost.* The words tenure and Poetry should never be in the same sentence. A poem that is almost as translucent as the edge of a slice of apple. The words

Professor and Poetry are at war. For the poem tells the professor, *burn the classroom walls to the ground.* It tells the professor to plant a tree inside every student's head. So it may bloom, like a revolution.

Follow the lines to the entrance of the gulag. What is it worth, a cup of coffee and a cigarette for a man's life? What is the weight of money when faced with the poem? The poem has dropped out of high school. A poem is not a college, but a collage. A poem is not a University, but a universe. There is nothing to worship like an urn. As soon as one writes it down, the poem changes. It is a spiral, shifting slow above us, a cosmos inside us, like the constellations, like the staircase of our bodies. You can never kill the poem. Erase the poem. The absence of song and the poem is still. There is nothing here about Capital. The poem is the first breath and the last death. It is as hard it is said for a Professor to enter the Kingdom of Poetry as it is for a camel to fit through the 'e' of Helvetica. A poem is not an Academy of Poets. There is no Academy of Poets.

Sean Thomas Dougherty

The Singing Wreck Of Us

"and misery loves/ her dog barking at a cloud which is the sky"
—Justin Bigos

Let there be whiskey & ruin, the rest will sort itself out. When we drag ourselves out of the dregs who cares how we stink. It's better to be with a friend on the nightshift of no regrets, even bored sometimes, with secrets sewn into our chests or driving down some county road, counting one's griefs like shots of whiskey and Vodka tonics, at an East Side club where the head of the transportation Union sips Martinis with the Mayor, & the dude you know runs half the heroin in from Detroit leans over the jukebox humming Alicia Keys, how did you end up here, slurred to the point of stumbling yet a walking razor even the bouncer twice your size knows there is something off, a big damaged & dangerous in your eyes, you try to focus on the space in front of you, her hand on the back of your neck, yet you feel you could die this night over nothing, in that way so many of us go, over something petty, a wrong word said, nothing more & then the chalk-lines out in the street. But you are instead humming, drawing yourself somewhere better & anyways this was years ago. Now the case managers come to your house to see the children, your girlfriend sick, dying her slow death. What else do I have to say? I speak in the second person so I can say it. That distance towards another county far away. As walking on the ice in winter, the blinding sunlight off the great lakes, cutting the hole, casting the line, waiting, and then the tug. The old men sitting over their holes for hours. What is passing passes like this, how in spring when the melting begins, the ice breaks, the groan & ache of it loud enough to fill the sky, sudden & then nothing more. The sudden fractures unseen until the shatter. Which is why I hold your swollen hand & see the constellations of the wounds in your skin & try not to make something more of them than pain, but we both know there must be something more. Something to lift up our lives & drop us down across town, or in a hospital where they pronounce you cured. But we both know this pain will only end in a formal light we try to forgive, and forget. To go this way is common as the light that creeps over the lake this humid summer morning, walking quietly on tired dog feet. It is too early for the children to be not asleep, I hear their tiny feet running in search of the dog. They pull his tail and chase him barking. I am not trying to say anything I fear except now it is the dog days of summer where we eat & sweat, and inside my chest is a church wall, somewhere to pray, or am I refugee, asking for amnesty? No, it is the now where we are refugees. Starlight even each evening hurts my eyes. If there is nothing beautific to claim from this life all I can claim for us is this your razored breath as I watch you fall to sleep on the coach, curled into a question mark, or the way our daughters play a game they've invented, they sit eyes closed, face to face & touch each other's cheeks with their fingers & do not say a sound, as if they are speaking their own secret dialect, almost purring, before one suddenly screams & pushes the other down, and they tumble, falling together, teaching themselves about pain, and how it passes, how everything passes—

Sean Thomas Dougherty

To Assume the Debts of Tommy Ramone

I want to find a new name for the wind, for the smoke curling
around her eyes in some punk club after hours high. I want to
rewrite each day after it dies, so it may keep us breathing
forever. The barbiturates of our mouths.
Push into the black dirt, lying in the long grass outside of an
abandoned farm house,
the soft cindered earth of our dead. When I die throw my ashes into
the Susquehanna or the Merrimack or the Hudson, or
something minor, a tributary with a name like Walnut Creek
which runs through the flooded wood to the Great Lakes.
Eventually everything reaches the Sea.
The Sea of We. I want to find one new word for making music, a
language which is nearly song itself, electric as copper tubing
joining our palms
into applause, or more like the pause right before the clapping, the
rising hairs on the back of our hands. Where is the name for
that? A name like a birthmark in a small town to get some fix,
A name to disown what has been done. A new name for the rain, a
new name for a cloud, an old name for the dirt. The oldest we
witness. Gripping it, in our two fists.
The house where we learned our letters, written along the keyboard
like a never before played chord we realize is a melody from a
lullaby our mother sang. What is the smeared name written
inside a matchbook? The strange scratching on the wooden
pallet at work, the letters you can read in the seeded grass, the
shape of a clipped fingernail is a moon and a word.
The fences between yards torn by children, a nightbird shrieking
blowing vowels, the tunneled ear of who we are, can you hear us
through the kitchen window. We are the voices of neighbors
arguing, the verb of the blues in the background of some dive.
They are breaking down the door again. This time for good.

Here come the cupboards rattling. They are dancing the Polka on my
head. What is a name for this game? This getting for what we owe?
The bottle long emptied. Everything is so small, insignificant, and yet
so commonly exquisite, tiny as a gleaming pill. The rectangular
glass of the lens, this one life, adjust the knob, to focus in on how
nearly. How nearly everything was. Then we are gone, like Tommy
Ramone, leaving behind this scar in the air.

Jehanne Dubrow
Manifesto of the Radically Uncool

Poems that have never lived in Brooklyn.

Poems allergic to cigars. Poems without a favorite bourbon.

Poems whose faces are clean shaven, whose arms are unsleeved of tiger tattoos.

Poems that aren't gluten-free.

Poems that learned to rhyme by singing along to Cole Porter. *If Mae West you like, / Or me undressed you like.*

Poems that watch the nightly news.

Poems that lost their virginity too late. The rest of the poems had already coupleted and decoupleted, had even tried tercets and quatrains. Poems that stayed monostich for decades.

Poems that don't wear skinny jeans.

Poems that aren't invited to the prom. They stay at home to watch *Gone with the Wind* with their mothers. They know every word Scarlett sobs in the rough skin of Rhett Butler's neck.

Poems that phone the cute boy to say, *I like you*—no matter that the only answer is the *umm* of the dial tone.

Poems in bed by 10 p.m.

Poems that don't eat artisanal toast or croissants shaped like donuts or berries foraged from a friend's backyard.

Poems that are bad at small talk. *I just got my period*, they tell you at the cocktail party when you bring them a Shirley Temple with extra cherries.

Poems that pop their pimples in the mirrors of other poems.

Jehanne Dubrow

Against War Movies

I see my husband shooting in *Platoon*,
and there he is again in *M*A*S*H* (how weird
to hear him talk like Hawkeye Pierce), and soon
I spot him everywhere, his body smeared
with mud, his face bloodied. He's now the star
of every ship blockade and battle scene—
The Fighting 69th, *A Bridge Too Far*,
Three Kings, *Das Boot*, and *Stalag 17*.
In *Stalingrad* he's killed, and then
he's killed in *Midway* and *A Few Good Men*.
He's burned or gassed, he's shot between the eyes,
or shoots himself when he comes home again.
Each movie is a training exercise,
a scenario for how my husband dies.

Fancy

Those evenings when they dressed for an affair,
     my parents were most beautiful, my father stiff,
so sensitive to the strip of silk around his throat
     that he barely moved, except to hold the door
for my mother, and my mother's neck a naked
     thing above her gown, the bow that rustled
when she stood, like a satin orchid planted near
     her skin. Her shoes were thin, sharp knives,
making a sound I knew as fancy, *click-clack*
     click-clack across the black and white foyer.
They pinched her toes, she said, which was her way
     of telling me that loveliness should hurt. Even
before she left, her hair loosened from its bun,
     as though something in her wanted to escape.

     I rarely heard them coming home after the waltz
and gin, ungloved, unfastened from the car,
     his hand resting on the small secret of her back,
her zipper finally splitting at the teeth. But I
     imagined them speaking French or Polish at a party,
holding the words so long inside their mouths
     that language felt like infidelity, made me look
away. Each morning my mother's velvet purse
     wilted on a chair, empty of its midnight contents:
ruby lipstick, tiny lake of a pocket mirror.
     My father's tie lay crumpled on the bed.
The romance of objects—both their costumes
     on hangers again, still clasping the scent
of two bodies that bent, unbent inside of them.

Rebecca Morgan Frank
Listen Up! A Manifesto

A poem is born in the ear. This is what I believe. A poem begins with an incessant tune inside my head, not unlike the ones we first learn: *Hickory dickory dock, the mouse ran up the—* clock-like ticking takes its territory and the echoes of sounds lead the way. It has always been this route to a poem for me. One of my first poetry teachers told me to beware of my ear: she was right. It is easy to fall into offering up the singsong prattle of a small child, making a tune to please oneself.

The problem with following your ear is that the ear can be lazy. The lazy ear gives us the nearest possible echoes of sound, the simplest reply to a call. Everything becomes a response, like a ball pinging from wall to wall. It's easy to not only lose the initial call, but to forget that you can start again, that every word is not a sonic response to the ground you've laid down. I work hard to make my imagination take the initiative and not just trail around behind the ear, handing it whatever comes easily.

One of the first poems I tried to write, long before the creative writing classes of graduate school, both reflects and takes on this conundrum:

Stray poems wander through my house
wearing my shoes, trying on my hats.
They slip into the kitchen,
singing of mangoes and burgundy wine,
or run through the garden telling tales of
lavender and dandelions.
They drum in the plumbing and dance on the windowsills;

they make themselves tea and invite all the dead,
who add their own melodies to the verbal symphony
that performs in my head.

Studying the craft of poetry involved studying the craft of leaving things behind, no matter how dear they seemed. If I were to take in all of those stray poems born by ear, poems that multiply and search for homes, I would become one of those crazy poem people, and it would be difficult to clean out the house and find homes for all, maybe any, of them. Instead, I walk by, maybe offer a scratch behind the ears. Frost says, "if it is a wild tune, it is a poem." My poetic struggle is to discard the mundane tunes and seek out the wild ones.

In my case, my internal ear is insistent because my external ones refuse to let the world in fully. Even with hearing aids, a portion of the sound around me is lost. Most birds, many women, alarms, cars, the tea kettle—they all leave me in a silent space to hear the tune rising from inside. When I teach poetry, I have students write a poem by ear: no paper, pen, computer: they just listen and recite internally. They hate me for that week. By the end of the week, there are always a good number of poets who claim they had been transformed in the act of composing by listening (instead of looking, whether at a page or, increasingly, a screen); often the whole class can see a radical change in their work. For these poets that respond to this exercise have already been looking, and now they have begun listening. Even in our increasingly image-based world, if we listen hard enough, the music will come, the ear will deliver.

Neuroscientists study prosody, and we know that language has meaning through sound as well as through signs. When we respond to a poem, we are responding in part to the song, which is an expression of how another person hears the world.

These assertions should not be confused with some belief in a muse that lands in the ear canal and conducts a poem on its own. The tune begins like a bee buzzing around the head, an insistent beginning that won't make honey on its own. Listening means not just listening to ourselves but listening constantly to the poems and poetics of those we admire, and sometimes those we detest. It means listening to the world around us, its varying rhythms, its injustices, its calls to insight and action. To listen solely to one's self is self-indulgent, uninteresting, and, as this is my manifesto, I'll add immoral.

My poetic manifesto can fit on my gravestone: Keep listening.

Works Cited

Frost, Robert. "The Figure a Poem Makes." *The Collected Prose of Robert Frost*. Edited by Mark Richardson, Belknap of Harvard UP, 2007, p. 131.

Juramentado

Bind the body in bondage to God—
the blood flow slowed steals

the quick out of the bullet's rip,
makes you unstoppable for that flight

of blade that smites the godless bodies,
a streak of dominos falling

from your welded touch.
A stroke of devoted luck.

The moving holy body perforated
by a useless gun guides guerilla warfare:

the jungle-buried bodies, prone,
your target, as your flash attack bates

the ineffective smack of bullet.
Bodies lie. Soon arms

were in evolution, a gun created
to cap this newfound spectacle:

a man who dies for love
of the afterlife, no country here his own.

Stories say a woman passed, bound
her breasts and spun through

town, like a whirling devotion
wielding the *kris*, its curved edge.

no match for the colt .45,
engineered to stop

the *juramentado*. The latest
weapon in the battle of gods.

Crawfish Chorus

Crawfish, crawfish,
Mary caught a dogfish.
Dog face, dog race,
send her down the Brown's place.

One, two, three, the roof's
done broke free: now
the water comes and
lifts us all up.
You are not it.

And the wind whirls round
and lifts us up.
And the wind rolls round
and puts us down.
Lightening strikes twice.

If you reach right in,
a catfish.
If you reach right in
a catfish.
Will swallow your arm
and spit you back out.
Swallow it, chase it, chase it
down with a coupla crawfish.
Craw. Craw. Craw fish.
Crawling. Fish.

Elisa Gabbert and Kathleen Rooney
Some Notes on Manifestos

The best manifestos don't start as manifestos. Nor do they quote lines from other manifestos. They emerge spontaneously, in one sitting, and are not improved by editing or supporting evidence.

Manifestos don't say "What if. . . ." They just say.

Foreign phrases can give your manifesto a *je ne sais quoi*. They can make you a *bête noire* and/or an *enfant terrible*. Don't try this if you're French.

Though it starts with the word "manifest," the manifesto is anything but obvious. It should feel like a kick to the body, but a kiss to the mind. Everything is about power except power, which is about sex. (A good manifesto never tries to relativize something absolute.)

The commercialization of outer space, the dragooning of animals into human wars—we are opposed to many things over which we have no control. Satire and great art flourish during dark political times; they make intellectuals feel better but accomplish nothing politically.

Neither seasons nor weather dictate pauses in a manifesto. Ideally, your manifesto has no pauses. Caesuras are a sign of hesitation.

The sweeping away of life's illusions resembles actual sweeping almost not at all. (But the death of metaphors is beyond the scope of this manifesto.)

To be prophetic, make bombastic statements and leap into the dark. Don't over-rely on cogency in the service of meaning. Do not abuse your audience with excessive chatter. A manifesto is all middle with no intro or outro.

A joke cycle consists of a series of related jokes about a particular group; as far as anyone knows, there's never been a manifesto cycle.

"Collaboration" should not be confused with "building consensus." Consensus, of course, is a myth. But we can all agree, can't we, that a manifesto should be aesthetic as well as political?

The job of a manifesto is not to get where you're coming from. The manifesto isn't inhuman, it just isn't human.

Art is not supposed to comfort you, but how do you know when it's the right kind of discomfort? Art should be at least slightly strange—a water balloon, but filled with vodka. Art should be at least slightly toxic.

This is not a painting to be hung above your mother's couch. A painting can be about paint but a manifesto can't just be about language; words always mean something else.

You don't recall particular lines from manifestos, just their color and shape. This one is austere and simple: a white-walled building in the international style; this one deep and aquamarine: an in-ground pool in a hot backyard.

It would be foolish to ask too much of the manifesto. But you can ask it to be itself, to be vulnerable, to be present. Just know that it won't and can't change.

A representation is not a solution. If you're a visual learner, however, by all means go for it. Write about the past and let your handwriting slant back; write about the future and let it tilt forward. Let your mind go and your body will follow.

Love or hate, yes; but indifference, never.

Beauty and truth don't need a manifesto. That is manifestly the most beautiful myth of them all.

Some Notes on the Weird

A sad spectacle can make you muse on death.

Poets use "strange" to mean "evocative"; to the average American, "strange" means "wrong." This is not a criticism. It's an inquiry into perspective, or what's a counter-culture for?

Weirdness is largely predetermined by fate. This is not say it's necessarily genetic, though weird may in fact be in your DNA.

When you travel abroad, it can be weird to find that the natives find you weird. Cultural relativism aside, some things are just objectively weird.

The color green is often associated with the weird. But the more frequent association is patterns: zigzags, houndstooth.

This is not a disquisition. It's an essay, in the antiquated sense of an attempt, a stab. Its weirdness enhanced by its barely apparent unstable authorial "I."

Everyone goes through a weird stage, and later, a stage of romanticizing weirdness.

The moon, asteroids, planets with names—this suite of destinations is no longer that weird. And one day soon, no one alive will find Pluto's demotion weird.

I am not your auditor. Go ahead, do what you feel like. Unless too many exigencies militate against your will to act upon your weirdest intentions.

Don't start thinking about how smells smell to anyone else. You'll only start freaking out about the limitations of knowledge.

There are no fixed entities, nothing essential—everything is changeable; isn't that weird?

Thinking weirdly helps me fall asleep.

Hogarth said the line of beauty must be squiggly—would I sound weird to you if I disagreed? What if I inhale while whistling?

The lab notebooks used by Marie Curie are so radioactive that only now have scholars begun to read them. They feel a weird high when doing so, like the placebo buzz associated with nonalcoholic beer.

Weird how the future never gets here. For endings, abruptness is better than dissipation.

Some Notes on the Male Gaze

One needn't be male to administer the male gaze. One needn't even possess stereoscopic sight. One must, however, at the very least have "eyes."

Is what we remember about ourselves what people remember about us? Do we live our lives toward our obituaries?

I can't help reacting to the constant impertinence of your big, doe eyes. What separates us from the animals, if not lust, romance, or even devotion?

85 percent of psychologists agree: excessive staring is thought to cause stupidity and sin. However, at least half of psychologists pursue psychology as a result of a mental imbalance. That and a desire for horizonless self-reflection.

Both men and women prefer to look at naked women. Naked women prefer to look at sylvan scenes.

Ninety-nine percent of gazes are eventually averted. The remaining one percent remain frozen that way forever. This is their own fault.

I don't know where the heck the word "gaze" comes from, but it does not derive from the Latin meaning mirror. However, vanity and lust are at base the same impulse.

Do not resist the masquerade. Masks are available for rental.

If you sit on the lawn and paint your nails, you look porno. It's better if the lawn's part dead.

We can't allow you any photos. We can't allow you to admire us from afar. So knock off the open and unabated unmanly despair already.

I'm not looking *at* you. I'm *looking* at you.

Hannah Gamble
Manifesto

If these poems ever end up in a book, then that book's dedication page will read: *"For girls, and all the men and women who are good to them."*

I'm always so thrilled to learn that high-school-aged people (usually girls) are reading my poems.

I was such a weird, pervy (though I use the term affectionately) little girl: always thinking about sex while also feeling horrible shame about how much I thought about it. I read choice pages in my grandmother's romance novels and was turned on by how the women always seemed to be trying to get away.

I was also turned on by Batman and Robin being tied up together and writhing above a vat of bubbling green acid, any animal or person who bared his/her/its throat, and the way the wicked queen would brush Snow White's hair before trying to kill her with a poisoned comb.

Now I'm older, I still think about sex a lot, and (finally) I'm thinking about it in my poems.

When I was in graduate school I was afraid to write these kinds of poems because I didn't want my brilliant classmates and professors to think that I wasn't smart (and when one is a woman writing about dicks and vaginas, romantic love, pain, and aloneness there is that danger).

I am never trying to be shocking or confessional in my poems; I'm trying to be the men and women that we all are, and to see what they/ we see.

Hanging Out with Girls

Hanging out with girls makes me lonely. There's so much of
no one is fat and that he was a dick for saying that
and she was a bitch for not listening

to you better. Looking at pictures
makes me lonely, too: The time we were g-chatting
but I was also crying, looking at pictures of Eric dancing
with his friend's mom at a wedding.

Someone asked me at a poetry reading how I got so
comfortable talking in between poems and I said
that once I went to see some musicians perform for a birthday,

and even when they were playing beautiful Chopin,
they offered something extra, like a little physical
comedy routine built around the playing of the piece.

I said that since then I've wanted to give people
who come to see poetry a little something extra,
and that me, blabbering, is all I've ever had,
to give or to keep or to be with on my own.
There's really very little

art in that. You'll never hear me say it's noble.
Or if it is noble, it's only because it isn't fun
to show everyone how little you have
and how little you are.
But no one has much,

and no one is much,
and everyone should know that we share that.

Somewhere Golden

One woman said
Clean yourself up
with a cocktail napkin, so here I am
in the bathroom.
Sounds of the party.
Sounds of one man
pretending he gets the joke.
Oh, he gets the joke.
He just didn't think
it was very funny.
I can understand that man.
The bones of Tom's hands
made a fist
and told my nose
a joke, which is to say he
hit me. The resulting laughter
was quiet, but
well-sustained. People decorate
their bathrooms
like I would rather be at the beach
than in this bathroom.
I'd rather be watching swans
mate for life. Well,
not actually mating.
Okay, actually mating;
you can hardly tell
what's going on. Unlike
pornography, or unlike
a wedding ceremony. Or, no.
The wedding ceremony is more

like swans. I thought
I was just watching two people
hold hands
in front of a candle.
The people deciding
to wear flowers in the winter,
disrespectful of what the world,
bigger than us, said we could wear
or eat, like the asparagus hoers d'oeuvres
insisted it was a good time
to feel like it was summer.
At the wedding I was quiet.
At the party I was quiet
until Tom found me
offensive. The homeowners
long ago had decided
I'd rather be somewhere golden
than in this bathroom.
Outside the sounds
of people making promises,
or rather, hushing a room
to condone the most public
of promises made
in front of a candle.
When I'm cleaned up
I'll find, if he was invited,
the man who played the organ,
or the priest who wears soft shoes
so he doesn't disturb the holy
spirits resting in the rafters
when he walks through
the resting cathedral,
stooping at times
to pick up flowers.

Noah Eli Gordon
On the Poem's Animal Sound

At recess in the sixth grade, I am a celebrity. I tell my classmates stories about myself, articulate the daring and exciting delinquency of my past. With each story, my celebrity grows. Soon, I've told them everything. I have no more stories. I am ignored on the playground, and so begin acting out again. This alienates me even more from my classmates, who come to resent my brutishness, to see it as a virus, which, fearful of infection, they avoid whenever possible. In *The Theater and Its Double*, Artaud begins with a lengthy analogy between the plague as a psychic entity whose contagion might be a matter of will and the theater as a sort of disease that carries a potential simultaneously destructive and redemptive.

Because of my classmates's preference for stories over the participation, even the passive, observational participation, required of witness— the theater of actual events, my celebrity was willfully deflated, cast aside, allowed to curdle into something dangerous, something unapproachable. Something adult. This something was itself a kind of theater, the kind which, as Artaud notes, "causes the mask to fall, reveals the lie, the slackness, baseness, and hypocrisy of our world." If, as Joan Didion famously wrote, "[w]e tell ourselves stories in order to live," then what happens when we've told them all, when we run out of these stories, when we have to live in order to tell them? This is the point where the chatter and babble of the adult world suddenly becomes intelligible. This is where the poem begins.

When I was about twenty, I remember sitting in my room one night, annoyed with something my housemates were up to, and a bit bored with whatever my other friends were doing. It was one of those evening where you just feel aimless, off-balance, agitated. There was something gnawing at me, but I didn't know what. Then, out of nowhere, a procession of sirens passed by my house. I mean there were fire trucks, police cars, a few ambulances, lots and lots of noise—sudden, alarming noise; then, nothing. It was dead silent for maybe a second or two before the sirens picked up again. This time they seemed to come from every direction, as though they were surrounding the house. But the pitch was off, all wobbly, a weird vibrato, like electronics trying to run on nearly-dead batteries.

The sound wasn't coming from the sirens at all. It was an animal sound. It was every dog in the neighborhood at once attempting to imitate the noise. None of them could do it quite right, but damn were they going for it. It felt simultaneously sad and triumphant. It was the exact moment I decided to be a writer.

I'm not writing the noise of the sirens, nor am I writing the noise of the dogs. My poems take root in the silence after the two have sounded: mimetic chatter and babble moving paradoxically from intellection to imagination.

Listen. That's a command, not advice. The poem must prove this: that it is no longer necessary to know much of anything is the noisy irony of the information age. The poem must waste the afternoon dismantling the paradox it took all morning to make. Like coinage or weaponry, the poem doesn't have to be useful or beautiful, but it must be. The poem must prove that a good illustration's the role of analogy. The poem must choose the event over the box from which it is broadcast. The poem must arrive at the problem of departure. The poem must prove that the grand narrative the end of narratives had had had had no grandiose ending. The poem must be a marker of the future tense giving off noxious fumes. The poem must employ the kind of choreography that makes one ache all over. The poem must prove that sun glints off a guillotine as easily as a gardenia eats it.

Between the house of realist fiction and a reel of film depicting someone reading, the poem must be a sort of alleyway of experience, a missing equation chalked on the blackboard destroyed by its own negation. The poem must reveal how cramming syllables into a canopy of trees elevates one above the hillside. The poem must claim a kinship with the palette, with its unintentional blending of the paints. The poem must burn the canvas and hang the brush on the museum wall. The poem must paint the word "lighthouse" on a lighthouse and in doing so prove itself deserving of shipwreck. The poem's habitual return to particular scenarios must speak of the desire to canonize the footprints it's been following, even if they turn out to be its own.

Works Cited

Artaud, Antonin. *The Theater and Its Double*. Grove Press, 1958, p. 31.

Didion, Joan, *The White Album*. FSG, 1990. p. 11.

For Expression

> Sing a song of utterance. I mutter to you. Sing a song of expression.
> —Gertrude Stein

For the feel
  in my palm
  of an apple
  fresh from
  the market
Against the
  viscous
  transparent skin
  of marketing

For the condition
  of air
Against air
  conditioning

For the brightness
  of the room made
  brighter by an
  illuminating act
  of the imagination
Against ingredients
  and blueprints

For the continued sweetness
  of chilled plums
Against plumage

Against the rifles
  the aggressors
  of elegant discourse
  display as flags
For riffling elegantly
  through discourse
  to display
  aggression flagging

For the curve
  of any Adonis's cock
Against a lecture
  on how to cup
  the sack while stroking

For the renewal
  of sunsets and moons
  seasons tiny saplings
  soups of all kinds
Against novelty
  stirring in the wrong direction

For patronage
Against patrons

For music
Against museums

For the body
  in its folds
  and dignities
Against collapsing
  garment factories

For love
Against labels

For workers
Against force

For the mask's respect
  of the contours
  of the human face
Against hanging it
  on a wall
  backwards

For paintings
Against frames

For pleasure
Against its conscription
  to a purely cerebral
  paradise

For standing
  however
  you see fit
Against posturing

For buildings
Against scaffolding

For the suit
Against the numbers

For the public
Against the publicist

For the sudden sharp beauty
  of seeing anew
  again
  the same
  old world
Against the art
  of money
  the artifact
  the art of facts
  and administration

For water
  that rises and falls
  the earth
  those on it
Against the pull
  of the village
  explainer

For weather
Against forecasts

For the cow
Against the brand

For Stein and Césaire
  Vallejo
  Sappho Rimbaud
Against Cage and Warhol
  Google
  Apple
  Monsanto

For the capacity
  to imagine

your nakedness
Against endless images
  of it

For the thread
Against the mill

For the attendant enchantment
  of a phrase
  tuned
  and trued
Against taking attendance

For enchantment
  in general
Against the generals
  of entrenched
  imagination

For the clit
Against the clock

For poles and zones
Against polling and zoning

For plasticity
Against plastic

For the poets
  grown old
  before us
Against their mistaking
  admiration
  for Eros

For a wooden door
  painted green
  impervious
  to weather
Against whether
  or not
  one has
  to open it

For options
Against operators

For photographs
  of flowers
  all over the place
Against poems
  where people
  aim telephoto lenses
  at one another

For pushing
  the last bits
  of daylight
  through
  the door locks
Against polishing
  your crown
  behind the curtains

For a girl
  floating
  for a few seconds
  across
  the parking lot
Against what's only

an ordinary
skateboard
underneath her

For the desire
   to walk around
   and around the block
   like a man who takes
   pleasure
   in circling something
   he knows he won't
   apply for because
   he's certain he'd get it
Against applications

For another poem
   textured
   with the sky
   night
   stars
   and the sun
Against its textual history

For the messianic
   and
Against the messianic
   and
For the freedom to be so
   and
Against the fastidiousness not to

Against Erasure

Tinkering with trace elements
or punching holes
to pry the copper piping
from your mother's insect voice
either way you'll wake up in static
which is like falling asleep in snow
Call it a tiny treasure
surrounded by a summer horse
& admit that there's a cup of coffee
inside every meaningful thing
you've ever said

David Groff
The Promise of Radical Content

Now that we've spent a century modernizing and postmodernizing, experimenting with experimentation, guarding our avant gardes, fragmenting our lyrics and narratives, associatizing and ellipticalizing and hybridizing, erasing and sampling and repurposing and prose-poemifying, we have pretty thoroughly rifled through the available formal strategies of page-based poetry. In the sprawling house of contemporary verse, our tightly held poetics have often sent us into separate bedrooms, doors slamming, with much weeping and angry night-long mutterings. But now, in the new century's morning light, we can make it new anew. Today, making it new means extending the range of a poem's potential content. The next frontier starts not with how we write, but what we write about.

In recent years, even as much page-based poetry has played with voice and form, it's often been happy to stay small in its subjects, pleased with what it discovers around the house, in the vagaries of nature, in the data of its meditations, in the perceptions of the private mind. Accompanying this constrained array of subject matter is an implicit, basically modernist stance that might have been arresting even twenty years ago but now feels increasingly like a reiteration of a cultural consensus. We've all long since agreed that life is full of disconnections and dissociations, and so is art; that irony is an element like oxygen; that our losses begin in the cradle and inspire lifelong melancholy; that each of us constructs a self out of projections and language; that life is feast and famine, and that poetic epiphanies can be pauses on a longer journey.

But thanks to scientific discoveries, political and social changes, advances in the understanding of sexuality, globalization, and a host of other factors, such modernist premises aren't necessarily gospel any more. Poets, being human beings, know this. But still we don't admit into our poems enough of our own, ever-evolving *Weltanschauung.* It's remarkable how narrow a range of subject matter we feel we can introduce into our work, even when we are people with broad and deeply committed lives, interests, and knowledge.

We have so much content within us. That content becomes radical when we embrace in our poems the public and private matters which preoccupy us but which we have walled off from our work because they don't seem poetic enough; or they belong to experts in the field; or they seem to shame us; or they're political, scientific, controversial, sexual or sexy, or too much fun; or because they make us squirm with delight or creative apprehension. But we can turn those walls into windows.

In a poem, we have the right to explore anything: Adult Swim, bees dying in their hives, Project Runway, the electrotweak horizon problem, Taylor Swift's man problems, lovemaking without power plays, the militarization of the southern border, scary microbes, the Twitterverse, people who see their gods at work in hurricanes and wars, getting an appointment with a medical specialist, dealing with cops when you are a person of color, the status of Pluto, nitrates, new ways to be a man or woman or both or neither, tattoo removal, plant sentience, Vegas. All content belongs in our poems.

Does embracing radical content mean that we fake it, compose hip, political, fact-filled, or faux-global poems that aren't in our gut to write? No. The summons of radical content asks us to connect our poems to all that compels us in our daily lives. Wouldn't it be fun to approach writing poetry with nothing consciously or unconsciously cordoned off, nothing disallowed? When we allow what is in our hearts and heads to infuse our work, poetry's great themes will remain—love, death, justice, the nature of language, the pursuit of whatever we think beauty is, whatever truth might be. Within those verities, we can find the language we need to bring into our poems the stuff that animates us every day. Nothing is unpoetic.

But what about the need to integrate our content with the rigors of poetic form? Shouldn't the two be as seamless as a rose and its odor, a rock star and her guitar? Won't an emphasis on expanding the possible content of poems cause us to forgo formal invention, beauty, and the delicious problems of language, and lead to an epidemic of poems that are dreary documents? Sure. Lots of poems will not attain liftoff. Yet new ventures in content will call for new forms, new ways to oxygenate our poems and make them take shape on the page—and beyond.

Poets everywhere are already writing poems of radical content, even if we don't recognize them with that term. Often, but by no means exclusively, the poets on the vanguard of radical content possess ethnic, racial, social, cultural, or sexual identities that put them outside the mainstream; they are compelled to include rangy subjects in their work because that is what their lives demand. These poets are people of color contending with issues of justice and inclusion, they are women demanding their voices be heard, they are international writers profoundly aware of the world's borders, they are queer people who will not accept denigrating sexual and gender definitions.

Yet all of us poets—no matter our definitions—can and do embrace the heady pleasures that come when our poems are one with the panoply of human preoccupations; when, as Walt Whitman would have it, each of us communicates the multitudes that we contain.

Embracing radical content will rouse our poems to go out and mingle in the world. If page-based poets bring all their daily passions into their poems, and believe they can write about what essayists, journalists, and spoken word or performance poets write about—and what non-writing human beings grapple with every day—then maybe we will all pay more attention to each other. And maybe we poets will find new readers, as we enter the agora and sit down with our compatriots over coffee.

Clay's Flies

I pull Clay up behind a dune
and yank his bathing suit to his knees.
We are new together, at high tide.
But before I can sink to begin and Clay
could laugh and protest and rise,
the horseflies swarm,
the feast for them as good as a carcass.
They pepper his body like buckshot.
Clay yelps, thrashes me off him,
rushes to the ocean's fortress of breezes.

I watch him swell with *sixty-four* stings,
the beach of his body rising in red dunes
I cannot balm or even touch.
The flies divide us (what, you don't sting *me?*),
but the blisters betray his health:
his system rises with reprisals,
antivenin saturating the capillaries.

Time flies. Our lives fall into step together,
our sex indoors, the kisses typical.
Then the allergies abate: Clay hugs dogs,
roams dunes, breathes dust,
all mosquito bites a fading archipelago.
It isn't love that quells him,
it is HIV, its slowed but erosive work.
The bumps and sneezes that I feared
flicker out like fireflies in the fall.
Clay's skin shines as sharp as a whitecap,
deceptively dormant. I wish him welts.

This isn't 1984: the virus, we know, is manageable,
at least if you're the class of man who strolls
replenished beaches and has health insurance
and is lucky. Clay burned through all the drugs,
his veteran virus resistant to every trick but two,
an experimental pill he swallows without incident
and a powder he mixes in a vial with sterile water
and then aspirates and inserts in another vial and then
injects with exquisite slowness in a twist of skin.
He does this twice a day, goddamn it,
then rubs the bloat a quarter hour so it won't go hard
though as a rule it does—it sets into a smarting cyst,
a node, a pain in the ass, gut, arm, leg.

When his reachable sites go sore, I'm Clay's last resort:
I scrub, don latex gloves, and shoot him up
in some place his pinch-and-jab can't grab,
forgetting, in my rush to shrug away the nudge of death,
to grip his skin, or squeeze the needle one to twenty.
(How do the unmarried manage, doing this alone?
They use the clip for chip and pretzel bags.)
Then, as Clay has tutored me, I rub the sac, disseminating
the bite so that the blood subsumes it.
Strange to touch your man this way. A medicinal caress.

It works, for all its truculence. The t-cells we once
knew by name now rise to anonymity;
Clay sneezes like a demon all this spring.
I could lick his mucus like nectar.
As we make love like old explorers
nosing our sextants through the capes and beachheads,
my fingers linger on his every swelling,
the signal of another hour Clay will stay alive.
Later, lying leg to leg and chest to back,

I listen for the flies. Those jaded undertakers
twitch in the nearly hearable distance,
aching to make their mark amid the marks we make,
ready for my love's hot blood.

David Groff

What's the Matter

As I lie dead on the hillock,
    an open invitation,
        my carcass garbage,

the vultures unashamed
    dive into their meal,
        a method to their madness.

They open their teeth of beaks.
    I feel them catch in my throat
        & share my callus of liver.

They score beneath my ribs
    to get to the heart of the matter.
        They must work to pick my brain.

My penis for them isn't hard.
    They mean to be only vultures—
        I am a beggar's banquet.

Finished, I stick in their craws
    as we take to the bed of the sky
        We rise and shine.

Cynthia Hogue
An Exhilarant Attentiveness

Moments when I am most exhilarated by poetry—whether it is
reading someone else's poetry or the process of writing my own when
it *clicks*—are moments when the poem is most *alert*, awake to the mate-
rial, and the beautiful materiality, of which it is composed. It is fully
present to what it's discovering in—and transmitting from—an inef-
fable source, call it the *ground* of the poem. This attentiveness, as Rusty
Morrison has aptly characterized such full presence, "can excavate /
rather than fill / the depths of [the] five senses," and as well, I might
add, the sixth sense. Perhaps Paul Celan had that in mind when he
underlined the maxim by Malebranche, that "attentiveness is the natural
prayer of the soul" (Felstiner). A poet can bring to the page nothing
so precious as this quality of soulful attentiveness, helping to shift how
we regard and listen to the world and to others, even to otherness.

Although I might resist a blunt and direct poem, I seek a poetry
that, instead of choosing to avoid something, *says* it. It should venture
all. It should be inconvenient or discomfiting or too beautiful or blind-
ing to read. To invoke Julia Kristeva's *Revolution in Poetic Language*, it's
herethical. I may have to put the poem that ventures all down, for it has
paid attention to that which I would—wouldn't we all?—rather ignore.
Perhaps, as an attentive *listener*, the poet has listened fully, and the poem
echoes something back to us, intensified, and we feel unavoidably
exposed. That's not true, we say, knowing full well that it is.

The French poet Virginie Lalucq has described the transmitting of that which we call a poem from mind to page: "The poem is cerebral. Its writing physical." I seek poems that don't exclude signs of their compositional process, their rough edges and their dumb and resonant hesitations and abruptions, even their disintegrativeness. I find these features dazzling, spare and fascinating, sometimes inscrutably daring. I, too, like the challenge of difficult poetry, the line whose internal folds or pleats are created by ellipses, the enjambments abruptly gliding off the linearity of statement in the middle of the syntactic unit. "Words are physical: words are nature and matter, order of place, changing place and force," the philosopher Jean-Luc Nancy writes of that of which poems are composed. "Words exert pressure. They go straight ahead of meaning, pressing at its sides: they sway themselves. *The poem is a swaying of words*" (my emphasis). I like the image of the poem swaying, whether in a light breeze or high wind. I seek a poem that is forceful enough to exert pressure on the world and into the world, to come out swinging.

> *sway*

Thus, I seek a poetry of determined indeterminacy that sharpens and blurs the poem's edges, illuminating like the halo of sunlight around wet leaves after rain. A poem's mindful discovery produces a laughter of heady exhilaration, with its dark, glad lining. Dickinson revised that Emersonian word, exhilaration, to contemplate the mind's various trespasses on infinity, which like the amber revelation of sunset, as Dickinson puts it, will "Exhilarate—Debase." The sudden awareness of the paradoxical *gift* a poem makes lies in the oppositions occurring simultaneously, arrestingly, which is the argument of the poem. The mind of the poem I seek trespasses variously on what can and should be expressed, and I find in that open-mindedness an attentiveness that exhilarates me. I am hooked if the poet's all in.

> *humane*

In the violent first decade of the twenty-first century, I cannot stop considering ways a complex, artistic mind approaches the phenomenon of violence. I've brought this obsession to class and workshop discussions of poets like Dickinson and Stevens, for example, poets who aren't the first to come to mind when we examine poetic responses to a violent world. I have been thinking that the abuse of worldly power poisons a nation's soul. Are we poisoned? I remember the Old Norse cognate *gift,* which means *poison:* the etymological roots of *gift* as dual and self-contradictory as that of *poison* and *potion.* The one kills and the other, made up of a bit of the poison itself, heals. If we *are* poisoned, then poems—with their precise and care-full attentiveness to how words are circulated, used and misused, in the world—are part of our puri-fication system. They distill out the impurities through what H.D. thought of as their linguistic alchemy. But a poem is not a lecture. A brash poetic observation, report, and judgment are occasions to think, to feel, but there are no *sides* in poetry. And that exhilarates me. That challenge, even that impossibility, to say something that presses on the world, that, as Stevens avers in *The Necessary Angel,* writing during WWII, presses back against the external violence.

I am thinking about the *humane* in spiritual terms these days.

It is the lack of the humane that obsesses me in my work at the moment. A poem can powerfully convey a view inflected by the humane and ethical, not as a definitive but as indefinable, thoughtful process. Poetry-as-consciousness, an approach to the world that questions the pat, official, or orthodox meanings imposed on horrific violence. Horrors follow unquestioned beliefs, as artists know. I am become something of a wayward citizen-poet, as Alberto Ríos calls an engaged poet (himself the best of examples). The poem I seek is in high pressure dialogue with the larger culture, may address urgent issues of our times in language that opens up rather than shuts out in its all-attentive amplitude: a poem of time and place that is timeless, and that displaces us out of ourselves into a more spacious and ample awareness because of its *care*-full atten-tiveness. With exhilaration, I imagine it urgently matters.

care

Acknowledgments

An earlier, excerpted version of "An Exhilarant Attentiveness" was published as a blog by *Hotel Amerika @ Motel Amerika* (13 October, 2014). My thanks to editor David Lazar for the invitation.

Works Cited

Dickinson, Emily. *The Poems of Emily Dickinson*. Edited by R. W. Franklin, 3 vols, Harvard UP, 1998.

Felstiner, John. *Paul Celan: Poet, Survivor, Jew*. Yale UP, 1995.

Kristeva, Julia. *Tales of Love*. Translated by Leon Roudiez, Columbia UP, 1987.

Lalucq, Virginie, and Jean-Luc Nancy. *Fortino Sámano (The Overflowing of the Poem)*. Translated by Sylvain Gallais and Cynthia Hogue, Omnidawn P, 2012.

Morrison, Rusty. *After Urgency*. Tupelo P, 2012.

Stevens, Wallace. *The Necessary Angel: Essays on Reality and the Imagination*. Random House, 1942.

in the meadow magenta

(*reading Robert Duncan in Haldon Forest*)

bloom looks
like lupine from afar
but up close the small bell-
like flowers of wild hollyhock

the holy that forth
came that must

come mystery
of frond fern
gorse a magic
to which I

relate to
landof hillock and

bolder the grayer
sky and wood
the straight flat One
between them barred

by the bushy Scots pine
medicinal veridian of ever-

green which though
gossip rumor spell
or chance change us
is not changed

Cynthia Hogue

On Principle

*I asked a Kantian, "Does this mean that, if I don't give myself
Kant's Imperative as a law, I am not subject to it?" "No," I was
told, "you have to give yourself a law, and there is only one law."*
—Derek Parfit

Is an act unprincipled
        because it's not subject
                to one law? A principle's
optimistic (the outlawed plan
        might not be under-
                taken). Also realistic:
it's will whether to
        do or resist doing
                something desired,
like a forbidden love,
        or deliberated,
                as the law allows,
like a necessary killing.
        The act could be refused,
                an error of ways, erratic
and wayward, the self
        lost in the moment of action,
                yet at the same time,
fulfilled. In mind,
        on the mind, neither
                certainty nor satiety.
Who really wants to weather
        the way a gobbled meal
                holds the body,
hiccups insisting on
        presence before the sleep-
                inducing tryptophan

of food takes effect,
  or believe killing could make us
   just, something other
than killers, or bestow a peace
  that may cometh at last
   because we haven't done
everything, right or wrong,
  we dreamed of, that
   arresting ourselves
being in principle a choice,
  though we'll never even
   now (say it!) say it?

Doyali Farah Islam
A Private Architecture of Resistance

A recent news article in *The Guardian* examines the prevalence and purpose of "defensive" or "disciplinary" (Andreou) architecture in some of today's global cities, including London, Manchester, Tokyo, Guangzhou, Hamburg, and New York. Architectural elements—such as metal spikes outside a Manchester Selfridges; concrete spikes under a Guangzhou bridge; and sidewalk sprinklers outside New York's Strand Bookstore—deter human use. More specifically, these constructions delimit the ways in which particular sites are used and by whom. They intentionally un-invite certain bodies and groups—primarily, the homeless—and, consequently, make invisible both these populations and the related social issues. That is, these architectural elements encourage the rest of society to disengage—to become unthinking passersby complicit and comfortable in daily acts of non-looking. If today's architecture cultivates an attitude of inattention, poetry both emerges from and fosters attentiveness. If present-day architecture is a public architecture of oppression, poetry is a private architecture of resistance.

When I was seven, my father used to play a listening game with me and my sister, in which each of us would be as quiet and still as possible for a set amount of time and record the number of distinct sounds that we heard: the refrigerator's buzz, a plane's descent to Pearson Airport, a birdcall, each other's breathing. Ultimately, of course, this listening game pointed back to silence in the same way that poetry points back to a stillness or a something-beyond-language. However, the game did develop an alertness within us as children. This kind of alertness both is and is not what I mean in terms of poetic attentiveness. To be certain, I ground my poetry in the particulars of the everyday; however, when I 'write' poetry—or, perhaps, participate in its making—the everyday is not what I feel transpiring within me. When I 'write' poetry, I enter what psychologist Mihaly Csikszentmihali terms a *state of flow*. All of the immediacies of my environment vanish: the hours pass without notice; the coffeemaker silences itself; and I forget to eat. The experience is akin to being lowered down a well: the deeper one travels, the more one is removed from the goings-on of the world above. What replaces sensory and physiological awareness is a deeper receptivity that increases thirst even as it slakes.

I qualify 'write' with quotation marks, because I am not convinced that the poet is the sole agent in poetic making. Certainly, a poet figures a poem as a physical object shapes a shadow, but the shadow points ultimately back to light—not to the object-in-between.

What is light, anyway? Life depends on it, and we see by it, but light itself remains slippery. It is the greatest paradox—*both* particle *and* wave. Shadows, and poems, emerge from and point back to such paradox. That's where poetry lives—in the turn, the tension, the ambiguity, the question.

If I were a fantasy writer, I would animate shadows—make them sensory companions. Leashed dogs, shadows sniff and feel the ground more closely than objects-in-between. Poems inspect our world with that scrutiny and intensity. They bring our world closer but also give us enough distance to shift our attention and refocus it. So, poems-at-work are poems that do not merely reproduce culture but, rather, intervene.

The idea of intervention—transgression, even—leads me back to a contemplation of urban life. Defensive and disciplinary architecture aside, cities restrict original and spontaneous movement and suppress the human spirit: sidewalks govern where pedestrians walk; and fences, bollards, and signs indicate that which is off limits. The emergence and popularity of *parkour* and freerunning counter architectural restraints. Although these two physical disciplines emphasize economy of movement, the psycho-spiritual dimensions of *parkour* and freerunning have less to do with physical efficiency and more to do with spiritual trespass through the re-imagination of the city: the steps, walls, and roofs of the concrete jungle become opportunities for personal expression and myriad reinterpretations of the urban landscape.

Poetry is that trespass. Writing and/or reading poetry enables us to reimagine, to reinterpret, to reclaim. Good poems leave space for the reader's unique engagement, and hearing and reciting poetry are valid kinds of 'reading'. Though a page poet, poetry for me is still an aural-oral art form. I recite from memory my favorite poems as I walk to the grocery store, to the bus stop, to the bank. Sometimes I even recite my own poems as I walk, and I believe the wind takes the words and carries them. I imagine the earth to be the greatest library—an archive of innumerable buried, scattered, lithified, and fossilized small-*h* histories—and I imagine the whole E-a-r-t-h reborn in each b-r-e-a-t-h.

While the personal stories in poetry are extremely valuable, poetry can also reflect upon and shape broader sociocultural histories. Indeed, poetry continues to play an important role in sweeping acts of political resistance. Poetry catalyzed and solidified the spirit of protest and revolt during the 2011 Egyptian Revolution and the larger Arab Spring. Elliott Colla argues that "poetry [wa]s not an ornament to the [Tahrir Square] uprising—it [wa]s its soundtrack and also compose[d] a significant part of the action itself." If we lived in a utopia, I do not know if poetry would exist. Moreover, I do not know if poetry would mean.

Beneath poetry's political usefulness, poetry serves a deeper, more existential—albeit, equally political—purpose which the word *resilience* encapsulates better than the word *resistance*. It is the kind of celebration of life that breathes in Naomi Shihab Nye's poem "Red Brocade" and Derek Walcott's "Love after Love." It is the movement not towards erasure but towards healing that breathes in the last three lines of Yusef Komunyakaa's poem "Facing It." It is the acknowledgement of mystery that breathes in Czesław Miłosz's lyric "Encounter." Notwithstanding poetry that may be out-and-out political or politicized, I believe that the most political characteristic of poetry is the music *behind* the language. This music is not metre or rhyme, but an impulse—a vibration—that the ear and body pick up as soon as one begins to listen in or to recite. One 'hears-feels' this music when, for example, W. S. Merwin recites "Homecoming." He speaks of flowers, plovers, flight, home. In experiencing this poem, I witness and partake in (a) revolution. Earth turning. My spirit turning. Yes: poetry offers a private architecture of resistance in which we can dwell and by which we can thrive.

Works Cited

Andreou, Alex. "Anti-homeless Spikes: Sleeping Rough Opened my Eyes to the City's Barbed Cruelty." *The Guardian*. 18 Feb. 2015, www.theguardian.com/society/2015/feb/18/defensive-architecture-keeps-poverty-undeen-and-makes-us-more-hostile.

Colla, Elliott. "The Poetry of Revolt." *Jadaliyya*. 31 January 2011, www.jadaliyya.com/pages/index/506/the-poetry-of-revolt.

the fishermen

for carl jung

upon the sloping green, the men stand, bared,
the old and young sharing ordinary
sunlight, their waists draped with cotton *lungis*.
there! by the water's far edge, an old man,
alone in his swim and drag, crossing through.
his white crown solemn and dry above the murk,
he is the keeper of the net—and hands

it over only when he's swum his length.
then each man moves, makes distinct his longings,
plunging into the weight and worth of carp—
most thrown back like salt over the shoulder,
swift disappearance into the deep pool.
hear the flurried utterance, see the white churn,
and each slippery body—a memory.

trip to yarl's wood

for the witness

her village is like a mouth unpainted.
she plots its edges, she plots its edges.
a woman lining a lip with colour,
she spares the henna of her body.

the shadow long in front of her is her
vision, and she pursues it—or rather
it pulls her body along the dirt road:
an animal plodding, tied to its load.

her thoughts and feet lead to women: new brides
whose backs arch like new moons, and the old ones
who still season the *ful madammas* pot.

a man will stick his knife in her belly—
see the scar like the fringe torn from a skirt?
! what a seed of sorrow and non-return.

Genevieve Kaplan
Attending the Poem

I wish I had a drawing and an object and a bone. And could better excavate the structure of the thing.

Do I discuss it? Not necessarily. The poem remains inside. And if the tree doesn't have enough water and slumps to the ground, I'll tie it up. I'll try again tomorrow. This is what I think. And know. If you sit outside, or close enough to outside, all the sounds come in: listen. If you want to see the tree bud, you wait for it. And waiting you'll be ready to observe so many other things—and have a moment to ask, how do you respond? what in here is reflected out there? where do you draw yourself? and through what dirt leave your marks? The way to begin is just to tell yourself: it is time.

↑ that part might be the hardest.

The poem is its own currency. You do not push into / onto the poem; you enter. You let the poem slowly create itself. You listen to sound above all. The sound becomes intention.

The hawk swoops from the tree over your head to the rabbit in the flower field, but that movement may or may not belong in the poem. That gesture may not be the one that matters. Like the small flies suddenly attracted to your breath—you have to test it all.

The poem never behaves in the manner expected, *or* the expected poem will be excised, torn, otherwise annihilated. I know many shady areas. I'm always looking for more. Is the poem a metaphor? No. I mean, I hope not. I mean, I didn't intend it to be. I mean, that's one way of looking at it. I write and I write and I listen to what comes before I think to form it. I look for what to hang on the branches. I listen. I think it is a sculpture that I hope will be alive. I hope it makes it through.

The poem is jealous of the tree? Slow-growing, wide-reaching, view-pointed? And I am jealous of the poem?

Which wanders in and out, which has control of the line. Which knows what attends and what / who passes. What / who stands in unseen corners. My manual tells me: the alphabet is one method of organization, color another, or size, or shape. In planning the yard and the height of the grasses: concern for what lands there, alights. If I misread, I misread.

For practice, for experiment, I took my practice out-of-doors.

I slowly set upon the product, which, earlier, had been difficult to predict.

In the interim, I re-considered.

from *Or / Ore*

Perhaps their stringy, gelatinous spawn is occasionally entangled /
    glued
on the feet of waterbirds, that action needed when crossing, first on
    the way to water
or later, on the way to flood.

If bears come at night and "help themselves," if we think ourselves
    "well-prepared"
for wildness, the words come out like something else, and something
    stranger.

Here is the note and the trail: we trade for food   we are willing to
    be uncertain until food   wanders in / appears into our
    meadow and scares   us to the roof, and scares us up   a
    tree. And wouldn't mind   searching out one lesser meadow
    (or one that is more   -er) and these some many   years in
    these   mountains from so long ago, steeped   in dream-
    noise and gathering and   culling that archive.   I added a
    certain thing, maybe, I projected imagination to it,   world
    a little narrower here than I'd   anticipated. Charge: to love it
    anyway and know its—revel in its—   subtle differences.

When the day begins, as it eases, and morning a battery and a
    billowing, knowing
the birds and feeling out their wings, thinking to leave them to their
    own—if they're wild
if adapted to the wild, do they need food? Would they notice their
    reluctant
attendant? With "its legs tied together in an ornamental bunch on
    his forehead" we know it is animal
and we know it is dead, and we know it is carried (by another,
    human. detail).

The evening, the singing: last in order of drive

The tick. The ink of it, and the bold stars
the planes' tailings left just there
in the sky, and so many waiting and wanting
for the same thing, that last interest (last
in order of time), asking to be made up, recognized
crushed, amalgamated, and refined, as metals
as (specifically) silver, which is second best, which
is the alternate. I give these two versions:

1. Silver. 2. Silverado.

And then the mountains and then the plains
and the gesture full of lambs and beasts
and bears—One gets eaten, one remains (1. Gets eaten
2. Remains). Catch its hind, its rump, then
what? The query. The tragic prediction (a moment
a moment, a tirade.) The perfect illusion: clouds
parted, sleeping in the breath, the fog. Making
perfect waves and perfect sounds, perfect
passings—pauses without division
or touching down.

He could not find the mine. We could not find
the house, we could not settle. (Reaching to horizons
for 1. Success. 2. Recognition. 1. Silence, and 2. Keeping
calm). So: there with it—the collapsed motives, norming
the deeper symptoms, yes please. And I'll share.

Vandana Khanna
My Poetry Talks with an Accent

My poetry walks around with brown skin and turmeric under its nails. It refuses to sit down and be quiet because it's a girl, because it has curry on its breath and hair growing in the wrong places, thick and dark. My poetry doesn't look totally American or totally Indian when it is walking down the street. It might have words that you don't recognize, that stumble out of your mouth like an awkward teenager.

My poetry talks with an accent when it chooses, and ignores you when you tell it to be a good girl. It knows good girls and doesn't want to be one. Good girls listen and do as they're told—they wear what you want them to (and never show their legs), write what you want them to (using pretty words), and love who you tell them to (never, ever an American). My poetry uses pretty words to write about saris and spices, about lost countries. It uses pretty words to write about being chased by boys with rocks, about faulty hearts that stop beating, about grandmothers who sing Hindi in your ears so you won't forget where you came from.

My poetry stopped trying to be "normal" even though it wanted to when it was growing up. Now, it might make you uncomfortable: you might have to look away or shift a little in your seat, you might pretend not to hear it or "get" it, which is okay because my poetry doesn't blend in. It will stand out like a sore in the room. It will be foreign and not apologize. You won't know what box to put it in and it won't make it on to your list of "approved" readings because it shows you a world where no face looks like yours.

My poetry is for bank tellers and secretaries, for exiles that can still taste the cardamom on their tongues. It's for child brides like my grandmother and teenagers who speak one language at home and another one at school. It's for those who always get it wrong and forget which prayer to recite and end the "Hail Mary" with a *shanti, shanti*. My poetry is for those who can't read ancient texts with its hooks and cliffs but trace its mystery with their fingers, wishing they could decipher its secrets and rhythms. So instead, my poetry writes its own secrets, makes up a new rhythm—full of the noise and music of an old world and a new one. My poetry is for those with a quiet voice who let the words do the shouting for them, who let the words burn on the page.

My poetry remembers: a country, a language, a smell. It remembers for those who can't or won't because it's too far away and they will never go back, because the hurt of letting go still stings red on their skin this many years later.

Echo

I cannot make it lovely,
this story of my father: his body
raw under the lights like a skinned

almond, surrounded by sandalwood,
pickled carrots, and the hush
of rice settling in a bag.

I can't help it, I need metaphors:
his body curls like the curve of a cheek,
a knife lies beside him, done with its work.

This story in metaphors. Not simply:
You lie on the floor. You've been cut
by two men you don't know. They wanted

money and you were too slow, didn't understand.
But rather: bruises braid his skin, the bitter black
of leaves, eyes red as the swollen sting

of chili powder. *Why do I write into the past?*
He smells only sweat, sickened blood seeping,
nothing familiar—not black and red pepper pinched

into the air, not the jasmine of his mother's
kitchen. Nothing—until his breath is like a tea
bag twisted, pressed into the cup of the room.

But it's not an Indian grocery, it is a shabby
downtown hotel, the kind that lock their doors
at ten, have security guards to stop the prostitutes

from coming in, from warming themselves
in the lobby. The kind where hallways echo
of accents. The phone is off the hook.

Not, *why do I write about the past?"* but, *what story
must I tell?* You lie there dreaming, but I'm
not sure, dreaming of your childhood in Lahore:

the city escaping the finite lines of a map, erased
by riots, civil war. You remember the hot nights,
chattering birds—how the world was never silent then.

You tell me over and over but I can't write it:
the same story, but I know we are leaving
things out. Embellishing. What they must

have said, the words, harsh like Bengali, you never
tell, the first cut and then the next, how you fell
like a sack of mangoes into a heavy tumble.

You have left the spaces empty for me to add
in colors, the smells, to translate to English.
To translate into the present, into beautiful.

Vandana Khanna

My Mother at JFK

Tries to pick up the cadence
   of the immigration officer's

intonations, blurry and abstract—
   quick turns of the tongue

stroke the air with all the bustle
   and weariness of this new world:

its thick accents and alleyways,
   gypsy cabs and jazz.

She learned English watching
   Audrey Hepburn movies where

every sigh sounded like music.
   Clearly annunciated vowels

and consonants stood stiff
   as sugar cane, as the British

nuns who taught her, who
   rapped their speech across

her knuckles. At night, she
   wants to wrap the cough

and sputter of scooters,
   the low moan of oxen

around her like her mother's
shawl, but she can't hold back

the sheer demand of horns
and sirens, of America

seeping through her mind,
until her body throbs

and pulses with its rhythm
and rhyme. It makes her ears

ache, makes her forget a mantra
about new rivers and old gods.

Matthew Lippman

I am not a scholar or a Poet with a "specific project." I have taught high school English and Creative Writing for twenty-five years. My aesthetic is an aesthetic of the heart. My poems strive to reach as many people as possible. So, my project is this—to create a vision and a music out of language that speaks to a mindful worldliness. Dare I say it? My poems are about love and mystery and family and death and joy. They are poems about teaching kids how to read, about embracing one another for being 'the other', about egg sandwiches and horseflies and reading at the beach. This is my project—to make the every day boring stuff, beautiful. The condition of being a human on the planet Earth with other humans on the planet Earth is so beautifully mysterious and these poems work to dance with that mystery. Once, I thought, poetry could not save the planet Earth. Or, I wondered, what the purpose of poetry was on the spectrum of the mundane. A few years back it occurred to me—in my high school classes—that the point of poetry was, amongst other things, to help build and sustain community. My high school students confirmed what I had been doing for years— writing generous, accessible, honest, and magnetic poems in an effort to bring people together from all different kinds of places. I know, it's totally humanistic, but I can't say that any other way works as well or is as fulfilling. This is my project, then. To continue to write poems that, in some small and minuscule way, help to foster a sense of coming together from an aesthetic and sentimental and honest place.

Something About Ecology

Everybody seems to be pointing things at one another these days.
The cop with the radar gun pointed his radar gun at my car
and my car pointed back, its rearview mirror,
to give the policeman an idea of what hurt looks like
even if you do deserve that ticket,
going 90 in a school zone during drop off.
Problems point at solutions and solutions back at problems
and even still
the white people and black people can't figure it out.
Justin Timberlake points at Justin Vernon
and no one wants to be left out
so the ocean sticks its middle finger at the sky
and the sky drops the hammer.
I sit down with my children and tell them to leave the leaves alone.
I want to teach them something about ecology
but I'm just telling them something about laziness.
Better off if I just leave the leaves alone myself
after they've fallen in October, stop pointing the rake at the foliage
and only if the foliage could point back,
maybe it'd throw its arms up in the air,
try and soften things up a bit.
Isn't that what they do anyway, daddy, a blanket for the lawn.
Cliché points its pinky at sentimentality
and sentimentality points back with two barrels of laughter,
three fingers of forgetting.
Today I wanted to wag my tail at ADHD but only because it had its
grips in me
so I gave in, went to the window
and shook
in front of the blue sky

like I had plugged myself into a wall socket
and couldn't find my mind.
When my mind points its mindfulness at the world
that's what I like.
I like it so much
it's the hardest thing on the planet.
The planet never points.
It just turns on its axis at x degrees—
a negative accusation in space.

This Modern Life

I miss my wife
because she's so caught up in her feminist texts on Moses
that I can't even see her face
when it's up in my face screaming
cut the cake cut the cake
cut the fucking cake
at our 5 year old daughter's birthday party.
Come now, Soft One, I say,
just put your hand on my cheek,
your lips on my head,
lets croon soft in the way that owls do
when they don't think.

I miss her eyeballs dilating and darting.
I miss the laughter inside the laughter
that could be two dogs falling asleep
or a tulip on a hill, yellow without a name.

I miss my kids when they are in the playground
and I am on the swing set and Jesus
comes off the slide kicking up a little sand.

When the little one smashes her head into a mailbox
and the blood gets in my eyes from wiping my eyes
to see the wound,
to suture the wound,
the blind leading the blind.

I miss dogs and cats and poetry and meatloaf and my best friend in
    his cornfield
with no pants.

I miss the globe I had when I was six
that spun forever after giving it the whirl
then stopped with my finger—Indonesia, Peru, Madagascar with the
     fruit.
I miss Madagascar and tangerines
and the business of life
that takes away from seeing that I am nowhere to be found.

Myself I miss except in the corners of the night, in the attic,
by the unlit lamp.
I banish the bills the phone the car the American Dream the
     opossum
that eats our trash
to another corner until morning.
I put my right hand on my cheek,
my left hand on couch
and breathe.
I suck up the nitrates and sulfites and rotted fruit of myself
and breathe.
I do it for hours.

I do it so in the morning I can go on missing the world,
to be the guy in the world the fetches the orange juice,
calls the clients, buys the grapes,
and builds the big house
so everyone who has a place to sleep
and everyone who doesn't have a place to sleep,
has a place to sleep.

Claudia Rankine and Beth Loffreda
The Racial Imaginary

We are all, no matter how little we like it, the bearers of unwanted and often shunned memory of a history whose infiltrations are at times so stealthy we can pretend otherwise, and at times so loud we can't hear much of anything else.

It's history and we're still there—there differently than those before us, but there, otherwise known as here. And that matters for writers. It matters because history's treatment of systems of classification such as race continues to impact our shared history and our individual imaginations. We would like to speak specifically to the racial imaginary that floats between us. It determines who we sit next to in public places, who we share our intimate moments with, who we feel we need to rescue, who we incarcerate, who we partner, who we don't fuck, who we question, who accompanies us to basketball games.

A lot of us when asked to talk about race are most comfortable, or least uncomfortable, talking about it in the language of scandal. We're all a little relieved by scandal. It's so satisfying, so clear, so easy. The wronged. The evildoers. The undeserving. The shady. The good intentions and the cynical manipulations. The righteous side-taking, the head-shaking. Scandal is such a helpful, relieving distraction. There are times when scandal feels like the sun that race revolves around. And so it is hard to reel conversations about race back from the heavy gravitational pull of where we so often prefer them to be.

There are a few other common languages for race that we'd like to evade too. One is the sentimental, which rather than polarize, as scandal does, smudges. The other is even simpler: the past tense. Because if we're not scandalized or sentimental about race, we're often jaded instead. This, again? Didn't we wear this out already? Hasn't enough been said, haven't enough already said it?

We don't want to substitute the jaded for the shocked, nor the sentimental for the jaded. Especially when it comes to writing. Our thoughts are founded on the idea that it's worth trying to write about race, again—in particular that something valuable happens when an individual writer reflects on race in the making of creative work.

Writing could be said to rest on the faith that there is something of value in witnessing an individual mind speaking in and to its ordinary history. This never stops. And it's not that the individual expression is, because of its individuality and expressiveness, sacred, beyond questioning. We're all disagreeing in one way or another.

We're not seeking agreement or consensus. But we believe in the beauty and importance of an individual writer speaking in and to her history with as much depth and seriousness as she can muster, especially when that history doesn't present itself as an otherwise-sayable event. And since race is one of the prime ways history thrives in us, it matters that each writer says her own thing.

This essay then is best approached as a document. A moment in time, here. A series of moments. Much can be gleaned from incompletion, absences, the detectable pressures on both what is said and what is not, and for those reasons too we present it to you as a document. Something to investigate, to both trust and question.

We feel the absences and the pressures ourselves very much, hear this as an instance, a demonstration of a question asked and then answered, however imperfectly or incompletely.

This thing we're calling the racial imaginary was shaped in part by essays and books by Fred Moten, Lauren Berlant, Robin D. G. Kelley, Judith Butler, Toni Morrison, and most of all James Baldwin. They helped us to see more clearly the literary moment we are attempting to document.

Two intertwined things about that moment in particular.

One is that in our moment, writing about race has its own set of literary and intellectual conventions that we writers sometimes use and sometimes struggle to re-invent.

The other is that certain assumptions about craft and aesthetics can and do warp the conversation among writers about race. These two matters typically appear in a complex, troubled embrace.

Here are a few of the tropes you would likely encounter if you started looking at writers writing about race these days. One: I met an other and it was hard! That is lightly said, but that is the essence of the trope: the anxious, entangling encounters with others that happen before anyone even makes it to the page, and that appear there primarily as an occasion for the writer to encounter her own feelings.

Another: I needed to travel to "meet" race, I went to Africa or to Asia or to the American South or to Central America to look at race, as if it now mainly can be found in a sort of wildlife preserve separate from ordinary, everyday experience.

Another: race is racism.

And lastly: the enduring American thing of seeing race as a white and black affair, the scene where the real race stuff goes down. Which is accompanied by the trope of the discount: the one that fails to extend to other people of color an authentic fullness of experience, a myopia that renders them in the terms of the "not really."

The matter of craft comes up clearly when we encounter the various tropes that white writers take recourse to repeatedly when race is on the table. These tropes are typically heartfelt; but their repetition should be taken as a sign. Here's one: "The imagination is a free space, and I have the right to imagine from the point of view of anyone I want—it is against the nature of art itself to place limits on who or what I can imagine." This language of rights is as extraordinary as it is popular, and it is striking to see how many white writers in particular conceive of race and the creative imagination as the question of whether they feel they are permitted to write a character, or a voice, or a persona, "of color." This is a decoy whose lusciousness is evident in the frequency with which it is chased. The decoy itself points to the whiteness of whiteness—that to write race would be to write "color," to write an other.

But to argue that the imagination is or can be somehow free of race—that it's the one region of self or experience that is free of race—and that I have a right to imagine whoever I want, and that it damages and deforms my art to set limits on my imagination—acts as if the imagination is not part of me, is not created by the same web and matrix of history and culture that made "me." So to say, as a white writer, that I have a right to write AS whoever I want, including writing from the point of view of characters of color—that I have a right of access and that my creativity and artistry is harmed if I am told I cannot do so—is to make a mistake. It is to begin the conversation in the wrong place. It is the wrong place because, for one, it mistakes critical response for prohibition (we've all heard the inflationary rhetoric of scandalized whiteness). But it is also a mistake because our imaginations are creatures as limited as we ourselves are. They are not some special, unin-filtrated realm that transcends the messy realities of our lives and minds. To think of creativity in terms of transcendence is itself specific and partial—a lovely dream perhaps, but an inhuman one.

It is not only white writers who make a prize of transcendence, of course. Many writers of all backgrounds see the imagination as ahis-torical, as a generative place where race doesn't and shouldn't enter, a space for bodies to transcend the legislative, the economic—transcend the stuff that doesn't lend itself much poetry. In this view the imagina-tion is postracial, a posthistorical and postpolitical utopia. Some writers of color, in the tradition of previous writers like Countee Cullen (a sly and complicated tradition, we acknowledge), don't want to have race dirtying up the primacy of the imaginative work; want the merits of the work made free by more neutral standards. To bring up race for these writers is to inch close to the anxious space of affirmative action, the scarring qualifieds.

So everyone is here.

Transcendence is unevenly distributed and experienced, however. White writers often begin from a place where transcendence is a given—one already has access to all, one already is permitted to inhabit all, to address all. The crisis comes when one's access is questioned.

For writers of color, transcendence can feel like a distant and elusive thing, because writers of color often begin from the place of being addressed, and accessed. To be a person of color in a racist culture is to be always addressable, and to be addressable means one is always within stigma's reach. So one's imagination is influenced by the recognition of the need to account for this situation—even in the imagination, one feels accountable, one feels one must counter. So a writer of color may be fueled by the desire to exit that place of addressability.

At the same time one may wish to write of race. And again at the same time one may wish to do any or all of these things inside a set of literary institutions that expect and even reward certain predictable performances of race. There can be a comfort, a place to hole up, a place to rest, found in that performance—that is, if that performance conforms.

But even if it conforms, the performance returns the writer of color to an addressability that at any moment may become violent rather than safe—may become violent if the performance steps outside or beyond those comforting conformities, or even if the performance stays within them.

Because the "favor" of largely white-run literary institutions is founded on an original, if obscured, amassment of racial power: they can always remind you you're a guest.

What we seek to detect in these examples above is the presence of a more general situation, the scene of race taking up residence in the creative act. This is what we mean by a racial imaginary, an unlyrical term, but then its lack of music is fitting. One way to know you're in the presence of—in possession of, possessed by—a racial imaginary is to see if the boundaries of one's imaginative sympathy line up, again and again, with the lines drawn by power. If the imaginative sympathy of a white writer, for example, shuts off at the edge of whiteness. This is not to say that the only solution would be to extend the imagination into other identities, that the white writer to be anti-racist must write from the point of view of characters of color. It's to say that a white writer's work could also think about, expose, that racial dynamic. That what white artists might do is not imaginatively inhabit the other because that is their right as artists, but instead embody and examine the interior landscape that wishes to speak of rights, that wishes to move freely and unbounded across time, space, and lines of power, that wishes to inhabit whomever it chooses.

It should also conversely not be assumed that it is "easy" or "natural" to write scenarios or characters whose race matches (whatever that might mean) one's own. This is the trap that writers of color in particular still must negotiate; it's the place where "write what you know" becomes plantational in effect.

We acknowledge that every act of imaginative sympathy inevitably has limits. Perhaps the way to expand those limits is not to "enter" a racial other but instead to inhabit, as intensely as possible, the moment in which the imagination's sympathy encounters its limit. Or: to realize one might also make strange what seems obvious, nearby, close.

Are we saying Asian writers can't write Latino characters?

That white writers can't write black characters?

That no one can write from a different racial other's point of view?

We're saying we'd like to change the terms of that conversation, to think about creativity and the imagination without employing the language of rights and the sometimes concealing terms of craft. To ask some first-principle questions instead. So, not: can I write from another's point of view? But instead: to ask why and what for, not just if and how. What is the charisma of what I feel estranged from, and why might I wish to enter and inhabit it. To speak not in terms of prohibition and rights, but desire. To ask what we think we know, and how we might undermine our own sense of authority. To not simply assume that the most private, interior, emotional spaces of existence—the spaces that are supposed to be the "proper" material of the lyric and the fictive—are most available for lyric and fictive rendering because they are somehow beyond race. To not assume that the presence of race deforms the creative act; renders the creative act sadly earthbound. We are ourselves earthbound. And race is one of the things that binds us there.

Crucial in what we're saying above is that we don't want to talk only of writing "across" racial divides. For we wish to also unsettle the assumption that it is easy or simple to write what one "is." Why might I assume it is easy to write what is nearest to me? How do I know what that is—and what do I miss when I keep familiar things familiar? It should be difficult to write what one "knows"—and if it is too easy, it is worth asking if that is because one is reproducing conventions and assumptions rewarded by the marketplaces of literature. And here again the racial preferences—the particular plots, the particular characters, the particular scenarios and personae—favored by literary institutions put special pressure on writers of color, threaten to deform what such a writer is assumed to know and expected to produce.

The making of art, is a structure of feeling, is something that structures feelings, that lays down tracks of affection and repulsion, rage and hurt, desire and ache. These tracks don't only occur in the making of art; they also occur (sometimes viciously, sometimes hazily) in the reception of creative work. Here we are again: we've made this thing and we've sent it out into the world for recognition—and because what we've made is in essence a field of human experience created for other humans, the field and its maker and its readers are thus subject all over again to race and its infiltrations. In that moment arise all sorts of possible hearings and mishearings, all kinds of address and redress.

For example: In that moment, writers and readers of color may feel profound and mutual anxieties that all people of color are about to be locked in, locked down, by the representation at hand, no matter who wrote it. But especially if a white writer wrote it. This anxiety is fueled by the fact that racism, in its very dailyness, in its very variety of expression, isn't fixed. It's there, and then it's not, and then it's there again. One is always doing the math: was it there? Was it not? What just happened? Did I hear what I thought I heard? Should I let it go? Am I making too much of it? Racism often does its ugly work by not manifesting itself clearly and indisputably, and by undermining one's own ability to feel certain of exactly what forces are in play. This happens in reading as it does everywhere else. In a sense, it doubles-down the force of race—you feel it, you feel the injury, the racist address, and then you question yourself for feeling it. You wonder if you've made your own prison.

Another example: white writers can get explosively angry when asked to recognize that their racial imaginings might not be perfect—when asked to recognize that their imagination is not entirely their own—and in particular when confronted with that fact by a person of color questioning something they wrote. And the target of that anger is usually the person of color who shared with them this fact. The white writer feels injured in this moment—misunderstood and wounded—and believes it is the reader, the person of color, who has dealt the injury. This is how the white mind tends to racial "wounds"—it makes a mistake about who or what has dealt the injury. For it is not the reader of color who deals the injury. It is whiteness itself. To reconstruct the reader of color as the aggressor is one way that whiteness re-asserts its power in its moment of crisis. It has been exposed—it must now perform weakness, helplessness, it must pretend to innocence, to harmless and undefended and shocked innocence, in order to "reveal" the reader of color as motivated by unsavory, irrational, savage, aggressive, "political" or subjective tendencies which have lashed out at the innocent and harmed him (this is how "the race card" trope works to disqualify the reader bold enough to call up race where it might not be wanted: the trope enacts its dismissiveness by characterizing any mention of race as irresponsible, an injection of race "where it doesn't belong" when in fact it inheres whether it's called up or not). The white writer was taken by surprise by this attack—how could she have seen it coming? She meant well—surely this inoculates her against any charges. The attack was unfair. And so we must rally to the victim. And thus whiteness goes only briefly contested. This repositioning appears to cleanse whiteness of its power, of its aggression—for who can't hear the aggression in "I have a right of access to whomever I wish?"—and says of whiteness instead "I have been unfairly characterized and misunderstood, I have been assassinated by someone who's motivations are political and who is thus disqualified from the human endeavor that is art-making." Thus the wound is paraded for all to witness, and whiteness gathers to itself again its abiding centrality, its authority, its "rights," its sanity.

What the white writer might realize instead, in this moment of crisis, is that she may well be an injured party—but the injury was dealt long before. The injury is her whiteness. By saying "injury" we do not mean to erase from view all the benefits and privileges that whiteness endows; we do not mean to invite an unwarranted sympathy. But we do think white people in America tend to suffer an anxiety (and many have written of this): they know that they are white but they must not know what they know. They know that they are white, but they cannot know that such a thing has social meaning; they know that they are white, but they must not know that their whiteness accrues power. They must not call it whiteness for to do so would be to acknowledge its force. They must instead feel themselves to be individuals upon whom nothing has acted. That's the injury, that their whiteness has veiled from them their own power to wound, has cut down their sympathy to a smaller size, has persuaded them that their imagination is uninflected, uninfiltrated. It has made them unknowing. Which is one reason why white people take recourse to innocence: I did not mean to do any harm. Or: I wanted to imagine you—isn't that good of me, haven't others said that was good for me to try? Or: If I cared about politics, I would write a manifesto—what I'm trying to do is make art. Or: I have a right to imagine whatever I want, and it traduces or dirties art to limit the imagination. Or: I don't see color. Or: we're all human beings.

Part of the mistake the white writer makes is that she confounds the invitation to witness her inevitable racial subjectivity with a stigmatizing charge of racism that must be rebutted at all costs. The white writer, in the moment of crisis, typically cannot tell the difference. What a white person could know instead is this: her whiteness limits *her* imagination—*not* her readers after the fact. A deep awareness of this knowledge could indeed expand the limits—not transcend them, but expand them, make more room for the imagination. A good thing.

For one source of creativity lies in the fact that each individual is essentially strange. There is a deep strangeness, an alterity, in the individual human mind, a portion of ourselves that we never fully comprehend—and this is what writing taps, or is at least one of writing's sources, one of its engines. This might explain the enigma of writing for so many of us, that the writing so often seems to know more than we do, that we are 'behind' the writing ("behind it" in that we make it, but also "behind it" in the sense that we can't catch up with what it knows and reveals, that it is out ahead of us driven by energies in our possession but not entirely in our deliberate control). This essential strangeness, this unknowability, is a creative resource, perhaps the creative resource, the wellspring of art that shows us things we did not know but that are somehow inevitable and true—true to a reality or a knowledge we don't yet possess, yet find in the moment of encounter possible, something we accept the fundamental being of, even if its nature shocks or startles or repulses or unsettles us (Barthelme's strange object covered in fur can only break your heart if you have accepted, in the instant of encounter, its essential being, even if you have not yet comprehended its strangeness, its other- ness). But while it might be mystifying how creative impulses and deci- sions emerge from somewhere within, that doesn't mean we must make a fetish of that mysteriousness. For that unknowable portion of the human mind is also a domain of culture—a place crossed up by culture and history, where the conditions into which we were born have had their effect. Part of what is unknowable within us, at least until we investigate it, is the structuring of our very feelings and thoughts by what preceded us and is not our "own," yet conditions our experience nonetheless. So the location of a writer's strangeness is also the seat of history. A writer's imagination is also the place where a racial imaginary—conceived before she came into being yet deeply lodged in her own mind—takes up its residence. And the disentangling and harnessing of these things is the writer's endless and unfinishable but not fruitless task. Another way of saying this: the writer's essential strangeness is her greatest resource, yet she must also be in skeptical tension with her own inclinations. Because those inclinations are in part an inheritance from a racial imaginary that both is and is not hers.

We want to acknowledge that we have fallen into one of the very traps we mentioned at the start—we are having a hard time talking about race separate from racism. Indeed, we're not sure if we can or find it believable to imagine otherwise, imagine a time when or a fashion in which race outruns its birth in racism and becomes some kind of neutral, unfanged category. And we want to acknowledge too: this is a nasty business. We should not pretend that our experiences of race are otherwise. As we write, as we read one other, the internal tumult is unavoidable. It might be soft or it might be loud, but it'll be made up of some admixture of shame, guilt, loathing, opportunism, anxiety, irritation, dismissal, self- hatred, pain, hope, affection, and other even less nameable energies. The particular chemistry may differ depending upon one's idiosyncratic mix of personal history and social location. For some it is nothing short of an assault, an assault no less painful because it is routine, an ordinary effect of negotiating a life in a world of people largely comfortable watching the assault go on, or at least willing to minimize its existence. It's messy, and it's going to stay messy. Because history is not an act of the imagination. Which is the condition from which we start.

What we want to avoid at all costs is something that feels nearly impossible to evade in daily speech: an opposition between writing that accounts for race (and here we could also speak of gender, sexuality, other enmeshments of the body in history) and writing that is "universal." If we continue to think of the "universal' as better-than, as the pinnacle, we will always discount writing that doesn't look universal because it accounts for race or some other demeaned category. The universal is a fantasy. But we are captive, still, to a sensibility that champions the universal while simultaneously defining the universal, still, as white. We are captive, still, to a style of championing literature that says work by writers of color succeeds when a white person can nevertheless relate to it—that it "transcends" its category. To say this book by a writer of color is great because it transcends its particularity to say something "human" (and we've all read that review, maybe even written it ourselves) is to reveal the racist underpinning quite clearly: such a claim begins from the stance that people of color are not human, only achieve the human in certain circumstances. We don't wish to build camps. And we know there is no language that is not loaded. But we could try to say, for example, not that good writing is good because it achieves the universal, but perhaps instead that in the presence of good writing a reader is given something to know. Something is brought into being that might otherwise not be known, something is doubly witnessed.

What we mean by a racial imaginary is something we all recognize quite easily: the way our culture has imagined over and over again the narrative opportunities, the kinds of feelings and attributes and situations and subjects and plots and forms "available" both to characters of different races and their authors.

The racial imaginary changes over time, in part because artists get into tension with it, challenge it, alter its availabilities. Sometimes it changes very rapidly, as in our own lifetimes. But it has yet to disappear. We cannot imagine it out of existence. Instead our imaginings might test their inheritances, to make way for a time when such inheritances no longer ensnare us.

But we are creatures of this moment, not that one.

Claudia Rankine
Train (Excerpt from *Citizen*)

On the train the woman standing makes you understand there are
no seats available. And, in fact, there is one. Is the woman getting
off at the next stop? No, she would rather stand all the way to Union
Station.

The space next to the man is the pause in a conversation you are
suddenly rushing to fill. You step quickly over the woman's fear, a
fear she shares. You let her have it.

The man doesn't acknowledge you as you sit down because the man
knows more about the unoccupied seat than you do. For him, you
imagine, it is more like breath than wonder; he has had to think
about it so much you wouldn't call it thought.

When another passenger leaves his seat and the standing woman sits,
you glance over at the man. He is gazing out the window into what
looks like darkness.

You sit next to the man on the train, bus, in the plane, waiting
room, anywhere he could be forsaken. You put your body there in
proximity to, adjacent to, alongside, within.

You don't speak unless you are spoken to and your body speaks to the
space you fill and you keep trying to fill it except the space belongs to
the body of the man next to you, not to you.

Where he goes the space follows him. If the man left his seat before
Union Station you would simply be a person in a seat on the train.
You would cease to struggle against the unoccupied seat when where
why the space won't lose its meaning.

You imagine if the man spoke to you he would say, it's okay, I'm okay, you don't need to sit here. You don't need to sit and you sit and look past him into the darkness the train is moving through a tunnel.

All the while the darkness allows you to look at him. Does he feel you looking at him? You suspect so. What does suspicion mean? What does suspicion do?

The soft gray-green of your cotton coat touches the sleeve of him. You are shoulder to shoulder though standing you could feel shadowed. You sit to repair whom who? You erase that thought. And it might be too late for that.

It might forever be too late or too early. The train moves too fast for your eyes to adjust to anything beyond the man, the window, the tiled tunnel, its slick darkness. Occasionally, a white light flickers by like a sudden sound.

From across the aisle tracks room harbor world a woman asks a man in the rows ahead if he would mind switching seats. She wishes to sit with her daughter or son. You hear but you don't hear. You can't see.

It's then the man next to you turns to you. And as if from inside your own head you agree that if anyone asks you to move, you'll tell them we are traveling as a family.

Beth Loffreda
morning

Some mornings I walk down the street through the red or the green light through the scattered crowds of people to where I work and I think here I am, in all of this. Some mornings I feel like I chose it, chose all the likeness looking back, or not looking back but instead just passing by frictionless, doing its loud quiet thing. Some mornings I feel like I didn't see it coming. Some mornings it feels like a limitless solid. Some mornings I try to skirt it. Some mornings I try to think of it all as neutral, there but something we all, likeness and unlikeness together, pass through regardless, no need to make it into something else. Some mornings I know it's already made already. Some mornings I won't notice it. Some mornings I wonder if my noticing of it is a way to place at a great distance people I don't like, or a way to place at a great distance my own interior state that I don't like. Some mornings I know I am right about us nonetheless. Some mornings I count up my sins. Some mornings I wonder if I stay in all this likeness because it makes it simpler to know what to do, easier to feel correct as I fail. Some mornings I feel repelled. Some mornings I'm what repulses. Some mornings it's just absurd. Some mornings it is still the previous day because I have been awake all night running yesterday's stupid lines. Some mornings are uncreased. Some mornings present a plan. Some mornings don't know what they are.

Cecilia Llompart

"Poetry is like grass . . ." I once heard Gary Snyder say. I believe he meant to imply that it will always be there. And indeed, poetry—like grass—is resilient. It has been around for longer than we can say. It is difficult to imagine the world without it. And in this quickening world of easy gratification and fragmented satisfaction, I am trying to be more mindful about certain things—to appreciate that we are here, now. That poetry is with us, here and now. As for its role, I cannot doubt that it will continue to evolve for as long as humanity continues to evolve. If we cannot say the future of poetry is certain, it is only because we cannot say our own future is certain. I do not mean to forecast doom. I believe in a great many things, and brightness is one. But there are, as ever there were, dark and troubling times ahead. We are tipping—if we have not already tipped—past our prime on this good planet. We stand at a crossroads now in the evolution of humanity. And it is entirely plausible—I dare say probable—that poetry has a profound part to play in our collective push to bettering things. This, among many reasons, is why I believe—quite strongly, in fact—that poetry is a right, and not mere luxury.

I believe poetry is medicinal. That it is the original form of protest. Believe in it as tool for social change, and as catalyst for a necessary awakening. I do not mean that poetry—alone—can save us. Only love can do that. But I have seen poetry reassemble more than a handful of broken lives—my own included. And if words manifest themselves and materialize the world around us—and I believe we do erect the very world we move through every new day—then perhaps poetry is a kind of supplication for a better world. Is a consistent prayer. And if we read it, if we write it, because we love it, then perhaps every poem is—among other things—a capsule of love. Taken daily, made routine, it can indeed make us better. Perhaps poetry has been lighting the way for a long time, and we just have to allow our eyes time to finally adjust. It is something like the candle we light in the surge of our grief. It is the vigil we keep, the act of lighting another's candle. It beckons us to remember. It draws forth hope. Because no matter how great the darkness around us, no amount of darkness can put out so pronounced a light.

The Barnacle and the Gray Whale

Said the Barnacle,

You enchant me, with your carnival
of force.

Yours is a system of slow.

There is you, the pulley
and there is you, the weight.

Your eyes wide on a hymn.

Your deep song like the turn
of that first,

that earliest of wheels.

Said the Whale,

I have seen you, little encruster,
in that business of fouling the ships.

Known, little drum machine, you
to tease out food from the drink.

Little thimble of chalk and hard water.

You could be a callus of whiter skin.

You could be a knucklebone. You
who hang on me,

like a conscience.

Hallelujah Girls

The planets champion peace and the papers
champion war—but in a forgotten town,
a hallelujah girl champions the marbles,
skips a tired rope, climbs a tree for a better
look at her creator. She sees the old people
that prefer to sit outdoors, she feels for them.
They feel the wind right up to their bones,
the wind that keeps its own council with
the barn, rattling the beams, singing through
the hinges, hounding the squirrels and inciting
revolt among the pigeons. But all is well in
the family of gnats—the peaches are rotting
to a pulpy juice, and then to pure fragrance.
A hallelujah girl is thankful for the sting of
a good stew, but considers the blood on her
hands, the small bird that was worth nursing
the whole summer, only to be found by the
neighbor's cat, the blood of the lambs led to
bait and slaughter by the local butcher, how
they bleat out a meek chorus all the way to
the hard wooden heart of the chopping block.
A hallelujah girl falls asleep counting dead
sheep, and enters her own lopsided world
of dreams—the bison so small they fit under
teacups, hide them there long enough, and
they will revert to their own personal ice age.
A girl so large she clips the sky, wears clouds
like milky pearls and wedges herself deep
into God's own poor memory, like a splinter
of sudden light. A hallelujah girl knows heaven

is a dry tumble in the tall weeds, the cotton flea
jumping high, higher than last summer, the boys
taking their shirts off to swim, only the one boy
blushing a bit, a blooming rose across his chest.
And that hell is but to see your own sorrows
marching in in shoes made of stone, the dog
finally coming home with that open sore, how
it festered all winter long, opening and closing
like an ugly eye, how it was unsavable, said
her father, who took down the mantle axe
and, in one merciful blow, lobbed the paw clean
off. How the raccoon got the best of the dog
after that but never stole from the dish put out
again, took pity, or they made a kind of wild
peace. How the kingdom of animals is like
that—live and let and live on. How so much
is like that—a hard bargain under a hard sun.

Randall Mann
Usually Against Ideas

1. In an idea-driven, big-think, think-big time, it's time to admit that I am against ideas.

2. I will immediately qualify this because I'm a poet, and qualification is what poets do, or I suppose should do—so let me say that I am usually against ideas.

3. Of course this is idiotic. We can't build poems without thought. Without ideas, there would be no lines, no poems, no adjuncts, no groupies. Then where would we be?

4. I am losing my point; I never had a point; I am against having a point.

5. This is the point: I'm not saying I don't think about things. I just don't, with perhaps a handful of exceptions, come to a poem with an idea that is the poem.

6. Largely.

7. Have you ever looked at someone's poem and, as in a summer film, you could surmise what the no-surprise ending might look like—redemption; medallions—while dodging the usual explosions along the way? Avert your eyes.

8. I try not title the poem with the main idea of the poem— then there's nowhere to go.

9. Unless of course it's the perfect title. I once wrote a poem about a question mark, which was about (for about read "about") questions and the look of the punctuation mark. I

didn't start with a fully-formed idea, just the shape of one, the curl of a mark, an inquiry about inquiry. I was no doubt thinking a little about James Merrill's approach to "The Black Swan" (I even mention a swan in the poem, to tip my hat to him). So I titled it "?."

?

is only something on which to hang
your long overcoat; the slender snake asleep
in the grass; the umbrella by the door;

the black swan guarding the pond.
This ? has trouble in mind: do not ask
why the wind broods, why the light is so unclean.

It is summer, the rhetoric of the field,
its yellow grasses, something unanswerable.
The dead armadillo by the roadside, indecent.

Who cares now to recall that frost once encrusted
the field? The question mark—cousin to the 2,
half of a heart—already has begun its underhanded inquiry.

10. In other words, all of this is subject to exception. Which is numbing, which is true.
11. I have been to a couple readings in cafés lately; young, talented, ambitious poets began with what I guess one might call mission statements, or project proposals. But then they read the poems, which—and it's true, I am speaking broadly here—seemed so, well, *determined*. Like the authors, the poems were in a hurry to get somewhere. I would have given my latte for a little bit of lightness.

12. I once had a line by John Ashbery stuck in my head: "Jealousy. Whispered weather reports," from his poem "Errors." I liked the mystery; I like the idea of mystery. I liked that its inscrutability felt like both the beginning and ending of something, but what, I didn't know. So, I thought, let me begin and end with his line, and let the poem fill in its own blank. After months of wrestling with what to do, the poem wrote itself.

Poem Beginning with a Line by John Ashbery

Jealousy. Whispered weather reports.
The lure of the land so strong it prompts
gossip: we chatter like small birds
at the edge of the ocean gray, foaming.

Now sand under sand hides
the buried world, the one in which our fathers failed,
the palm frond a dangerous truth
they once believed, and touched. Bloodied their hands.

They once believed. And, touched, bloodied their hands;
the palm frond, a dangerous truth;
the buried world, the one in which our fathers failed.
Now sand under sand hides

at the edge of the ocean: gray, foaming
gossip. We chatter like small birds,
the lure of the land so strong it prompts
jealousy. Whispered weather reports.

13. So, if the problem is poetry, the solution is not thinking too hard. And manifestos aren't really manifestos anymore: they're tarted-up life-hacks. This is mine.

Corey Marks
The Wily Narrative

Narrative poetry has a fairly tarnished reputation at this moment, though there are certainly staunch defenders of the mode. Poems that tell stories can seem too easy, too anecdotal, too plain and unsurprising. Too blind in their assumptions about experience. Too ensnarled with confessional impulses. Tame. Unambitious. Out of touch with our moment. Fusty. I share some of these qualms. I've certainly read any number of narrative poems that doggedly trot out realistic stories that seem largely indebted to the writers' own lives, and that feel predictable, inert, largely untransformed. Why is it that so many contemporary narrative poems are marked this homespun, talky realism? Why do so many fail to take risks? Too often these poems lack the enlivening pressure of imagination and intelligence. At their worst, they fall into a laxness of storytelling and a flatness of language that dulls and squanders the potential power and surprise of story rendered in poetry.

The narrative poems that I most admire intensify their effects by breaking free from narrative expectations. They amplify or interrupt or transform story with another structural impulse—meditation. In these poems, narrative progression is countered by a seeming loss of control. The poems veer in unexpected directions, dramatizing the movement of a mind behind or within or outside—and reacting to—the story. In so doing, these poems, to varying degrees, make narrative an element that meditation draws into its own larger movement. Story informs the structure, but meditation governs it.

I refuse to cede story simply because it has been poorly handled in other poems, or because it seems a vestige of what poetry once was that many feel should be rejected in favor of the-new-and-the-now's habit for disjunction without resistance. When I write, I want my poems to be charged by the volatile fraying and rewiring of story and thought. Story creates the particular circumstances for the poem's speculation, and the subsequent unfurling meditation relies on abstract discourse, argument, figuration, complaint, and ecstatic cry. It draws memories, events, and even disparate stories into dialogue with one other. The meditation can come to a resolution, lead to an unwanted realization, or remain unresolved, still troubling the course of the poem's thought. Whatever the conclusion, the meditation must have energy impelled by the emotional situation, an intelligence that faces the situation, and an imagination that transforms it. The meditation should enact a mind thinking about, or even beyond, the story told, so that the poem can become larger, stranger, more imaginative, more ambitious. More wily, and, as a result, more powerful.

Corey Marks

The Black Bear at Closing

The bear presses her shoulder to the glass
of her enclosure in the bluing light
and looks into her habitat, the rutted path,

the cement-bowl pond rimmed with muck,
the red ball lolled against a log—
a creature done with being gawked.

You knock the glass. A primal indifference
twitches her matted back. Elsewhere,
the exhibits clear, children trail the trauma

of their voices through the turnstiles
as evening wallows in their wake.
Some garish bird clocks out the day.

The bear slouches in shadow, ridiculous
and vaguely human, and you lean closer,
nothing more than attention's ghost.

One paw fidgets idly at her knee.
The bears you came to see as a child
must be dead. Not the ones in books

you read, though, that were never alive—
they'd come back if you wanted them. The dead
stay dead. You peer at your own hands,

how they fold and pucker into mouths. *Kiss off,*
the little lips tell each other, toothless
and cruel. Above, loudspeakers announce

what they always announce at this hour.
It hasn't occurred to the guard that you'll be here,
pressed to your own side of the glass,

inches from the bear drawn into herself
as though you're not here, her black fur splayed
against the same transparency resisting your touch.

Wait long enough and curiosity becomes trespass,
like watching a woman in a restaurant
nudge the blunt nub of her nipple

into an infant's mouth to quell an inconsolable
anger. See how the black bear stares
into her paw upturned now in the sprawl of her lap

with the preoccupation of a reader.
Your mother used to read with that intensity—
it bristled a thicket around her. *Mother,*

Mother! Some other voice had her ear,
calling her another direction, into wilderness.
No trail you knew led there. She held

her grief the same way, paged through
as though the loss was a story
she wandered into child-like and alone.

The empty bowl was for her, the broken chair—
remnants to be claimed, sorted, dog-eared.
You left her there. The door closed

like an opening book when you went outside
to skirt the edge of a woods and thrash
the understory with a broken stick.

Three Bridges

When the rains came I was, for my own purposes,
on the far side of the river. Who could've known
the drizzle would ratchet to torrent, or the river
unbuckle, swallow its banks, ring the scattered trees

like so many necks trying to stay afloat, strip boats
from their moorings and batter them out of the river's throat
into the mouths of other rivers? Or that it would wash out

the town's three bridges: the one too narrow to walk
two abreast, the one beyond the last houses, already ruined,
abandoned by all but reckless boys and swallows,

even the one, story goes, someone made a pact
with the devil to build, the one I crossed in the morning
as it arched in the uneasy air like a wing.

And by the time I had to leave what I'd come to do
half-done, the rain made it hard to see, coming down
and never done with falling. Everything bleared,

went pale and indistinct. My clothes weighed
as much as a child. I fell, and the rain struck me
clean. I lost my way and found a river I didn't recognize

in its frenzy, whitecaps shearing its surface like teeth.
Even when the rains died, the flood kept on, worrying
the absent bridges, the water thick with silt, its current
full of animals coiled in the rush. I couldn't dare it.

Where's the devil when his deal falls through
its own reflection? Now the bridge is half of what it was,
reversed in the river bottom leading nowhere

I want to go. At least from here I can see my house,
my daughter when she walks into the yard with a pail.
She looks up by chance, and though she must wonder

what's become of me, she doesn't see my waving arm,
an unrecognizable motion in a landscape she knows
she should know but doesn't anymore. Or she sees me
in too many places to keep track; I'm the one missing

thing missing everywhere. But then her eyes catch
on the swallows sweeping the bloated river—no way
back to their roosts now, they lift away to take an eyeful
of everything that isn't what it was. And move on . . .

This must be what death is like: those left behind
look up sometimes where they think you should be,
but if they see you at all it's from too far to make sense

of what you've become—a color bled briefly
into sight through a whirl of silt. And then—who can
blame them, there's so much to do to reclaim the house,
to live in it again—they look away, and you're left

waiting for the river to settle back between the banks
that held it in place all your life and become itself again.

Joyelle McSweeney
Rose Cum Manifesto

> *Pero, Rosa es el nombre secreto de mi raza.*
> *La tarde caía como si fuera un siglo.*
> —Marosa di Giorgio

I am seized up and transcepted by the power of Art, an occult force like an occult bleed, obscene because it should remain hidden yet comes into view, dragging all sorts of buried material with it, ragged, burned and obscure: *sub rosa. Subcommandante Rosa.* When Art routes me, when it pierces my abdomen, it leaves a wound, the wound is a rose, bleeding through my t-shirt like a final girl's, but non-final, replicable, repeating like a stuttering remainder all over the globe.

The Rose is a wound, Art's insignia, it is an emitter like the rose-cum–radio-antennae at the top of the Eiffel Tower which drove the Modernists mad, a total location.

The Rose can cum, and when it cums out comes white worms, which grub on air and bore into men's hearts.

The Rose wants Vengeance for the crimes of men, for the murder of girls, for the rape of the vulnerable, for the depredations of capitalism, militarism, imperialism and paternalism, up to and including the total crime which goes by the name, Anthropocene.

I call it Vengeance when the Rose cums.

*

Every schoolgirl knows that Art is paradox, an irrational material, it runs on contradictions and insists on an impossible *and/or*. The *and/or* is a powerful mode because it will not settle either into a nicely-behaved hybrid or a mathy binary, but is at war with itself, a giggly, dire war, fought with dragons and hair extensions in unsafe working conditions; it passes through the bloodbrain membrane; uvular; its virgule tilted like a wig. It blinkers like an ill-set fuse, and communicates unstable, irregular bolts of current. Lightning strikes this way, and lightening. It shorts the appliance and chokes the child; it propagates a massive fake blonde who prints the century with her counterfeit currency. This impossible *and/or* mounts a sublime force, at once a summit and a declivity, a blacklight, a lashing of inutility which could light revolutions or reanimate the dead or smoke on the steps with her friends—

stopping the clocks, like

Au bout du petit matin . . .

or

Spriinnnnnng Breakkk Forrrr—

I have never been a blonde. We have never been modern. I have always been standing in fire, my hair in bloom, a Rose penumbra. I have always worshipped the disk of the sun. I have just dropped this bottle of attar of Rose. I have always worn this detachable pharaoh's beard, this chancre on my breast. That's for cancer, a common Rose, and at noon a tiny president comes out to speak in the garden of my balconette bra. Comes out to deny all charges. I stand behind him like a gorgon and smoke. Hot snaky curls.

Noone smokes anymore!

—Not noone but me and my baby!

But underneath all this flesh I am feeding [my baby; Rose] on bone meal, ill-advisedly, we've caught a brain fever, a prion disease. Rose madder. Like Priam of Troy, slain on his altars, it alters me, it makes my brain bleat, pleat wrong, my screen freeze, it converts me to Rose purposes.

To burn always with this—

To be done away with—

My [face] pressed up against the [face] of the Rose—

& 24-hr drive thru—

*

From Eiffel's acrylic tips to the harbor of Montevideo. Invert the poke in your throat, now it's a dredge to pump sludge. Now it's a platform. Keep it down. Then keep it up. It cuts coming and going—Art does. Black liquor, it made you sicker than your sister but it made your engine bloom. Skylicker. Ghoat song. Eyeliner. Black cow. With the disk of the sun between her horns. Black Dahlia. With the [face] of the Rose between her [face].

*

When the Rose cums I call

Whiteout. Blackout. 24hr blackout blonde.

*

Surrealism, like the lining of a purse you find in the bottom of the closet in your rental apartment, black underwear, a five dollar bill inside. Decat the bag. Insideout it. Decant its ducats. It ain't used up yet. Surrealism's a weird cell that keeps splitting, a cheese that spoils, bank that's split like a lip, a stormcell shedding black irradiant light. Chase it in your minivan under your blond extensions. Smash smash, rural hamlet, trailer park, the vinyl siding, burn mark. Mayakovsky died, the Futurists died into bureaucrats, Eluard died, but Surrealism blousons the sky, a failing, a dump of toxic tailings, a waste site, a black and deranged grain of something that comes up from the guts—*de profundis*—and slicks the universe with its Real Talk. *I call it Vengeance when the* Throat cut. Oil wells on fire. Assault on the school library: Obscene. That which should not be but makes a scene. Drink up all the current at once and all the humors: choleric, melancholic, supine, saturnine. Vomit it till it makes a soupy garment.

Rage in place of argument.

Keep performing this pageant.

Don't let it get buried [again].

Wear Art on the outside.

*

Instead of psychology I have chemistry. Instead of apologia I have poison, violence, verrucas, Vera Cruz, charcoal solution, a substrate, pine tar, vengeance, vitiation, viciousness, inanition, sweat, and dyed hair; hardened synthetic estrogens that work like a cup of trembling and curl your eyehairs, permanently, Bisphenol, pospholipids, jet fuel, Novocain, uppers, interrogation enhancers. I have a baccalaureate in botulinum, I can be harvested like a rose garden which blooms in chancres. I wear cancer like a badge, I pilot a garbage barge, our lady's brigade, a brigand, nose up the purse seine, the river on fire. Gut me, liposuck me, drain me off, set fire to my emissions—and out comes the Art:

> *is stuffed, the earth,*
> *with murdered girls*
> *make it hurl them*
> *back on air*

a spill of pearls
a pack of gulls
back to life
with blackened hair
to gust on storms
the poets love
to feed on trash
to wear the Rose
behind each decomposing ear
from each singed eye
a black gaze goes
like a lazer, drone or doe
and burns a mark
where it alights
The livid Rose
is food for worms
& is a worm
& feeds on flesh
& lifts the axe
that split its skull
& splits the waves
like spilt out milk
& storms the beach
& militates
& gives the nestlings
sweet relief
& liberates the bombing range
brothel sweatshop holding cell
Bikini Jeju Vieques
with the lit tip of its cigarette
it writes onto night's retina
Art's inflamed insignia:
the cherry Rose

Excerpt from "The Contagious Knives" [1]

BRAILLE (*he literally wipes the smile off his face; is in love with his double*)
Bradley Mannikin, my hypnotist double,
my hiccupping download, my credit card debt;
my event; my embedded chip; my embedded
reporter with his lens split wide, and now his legs,
and now his lip; erotically, heroically, scatologically,
similar; that is, like; that is, like this, a likeness;
the boy next store, except; would that we were
Siamesed twins, and could return to Old Siam
for a verdant romp and ride on the rickshaw: I'll stitch
myself to your chest. You play the rich Chinese lover;
I'll play the ingénue in her cabaret shoes in French;
I'll play the hand-me-down vamp. Cover my knuckles
with rings like eyes. Fat diamonds. Kohl, coal. And I'll give
you a thousand kisses and smack on the cheek
and in the eye: a power vamp. Amp to the chest.
Defibrillate, resuscitate, advance: zombie music,
Lub dub. These things are for sail, these things are a hit
at the port, down on all fours on the deck, these things
on the ship's log are manifest; which can be shipwrecked,
black boxed, indexed, finders keepers, law of the see:
when this you see remember: No Indian giving, no taking it
    back,
except when you take it from me,
Indian, Chinaman, Brad-lee,
no man is an eyeland, everyman must come to port
or ride the continental railway or nail ties; you're bleeding from
    the eye;
you're naked at roll call; you've been demoted; you're
underground,

underfed and listless, you watch your retinas detach, catch
the popfly, sleep inside the poptab or the synapse, dream
of a ballpark throwup popcorn on the jumbotron; kiss cam:
appear, appear, grey gnat; kid-lithograph; self-engraving;
wax-caste; sans toothpaste, sans cotton, totally unrecognizable
as an American; I receive your transmission, I develop you in
    my bath;
red light, red light; I wear the sailor suit I wore in life,
yes, like a Tsarevich, yes, and my pearl button eyes,
and my ligaments and stretchers like a cat-o-nine,
yes, one for every bullet I caught in CGI, this suit
cuts into me, cuts a fine figure, and yes,
now I wander the magasins and empty a magazine, yes,
into the bust of, and yes, into the right eye, I punch
your ticket, I trash the Louvre, and now I arrive as from the
    Ballets Russes,
from the last century's caboose, and, yes, like a kid Nijinsky,
I arrive, I come alive, I contract and percuss, suppurate and pus;
like a pageboy, I turn the page; like a cancer I take the stage;
like a monk I see the flashbulb bloom like a nacreous lily
and like the moon in the ocean liner's wake I foam and rage
and like napalm and cocaine and mercy and mercury I
down can rain.

Bradley Manning, I'll find you. I'm coming down the drain.

Notes

1. This poem was written just before the trial of Chelsea Manning, when she was still
identifying publicly as 'Bradley.' The poet retains the appellation 'Bradley' to mark the
poem as an artifact of this specific historical moment—historical jetsam, a dead letter.

Erika Meitner
Some Notes Toward A Manifesto

"A way of speaking this received language transforms it into a song
of resistance . . ."
—Michel de Certeau, from *The Practice of Everyday Life*

I was just on Facebook where someone put out a call for poems that
make a statement about whether graffiti is art or illegal activity. I fall
solidly in the art camp, mostly because I grew up in New York in the
'70s and '80s, when graffiti was one of the best things about the city.
Riders waiting on platforms would occasionally applaud when especially
colorful subway cars pulled into the station.

Lauren Bacall's recent *New York Times* obituary ends with her quoted
as saying, "I spent my childhood in New York, riding on subways and
buses. And you know what you learn if you're a New Yorker? The world
doesn't owe you a damn thing."

The world doesn't owe us a damn thing, but most of the time it pro-
vides material that makes for good poems. These synchronicities occa-
sionally come like neatly delivered Amazon packages. Alternately, and
more often, they have to be unearthed with some effort, like an especially
stubborn potato shoehorned from a garden. Then there are the floods,
the twisted metal, the black holes, the rubble, the ashes, the hatred, the
unexpected loss—the things we don't want and don't ask for—ruinous,
tragic, rage-inducing, they can paralyze us or move us to action.

A manifest is a ship's record of passengers—an accounting of travel-
ers; or in the case of catastrophe, either a catalogue of those who were
lost, or a roll call of survivors. A manifesto as a list, a way to bear witness.

In Judaism, we say *naaseh v'nishma*—which means, loosely, *do first, understand later*. It's a call to action over intention, a motto of practice over perfection—the idea that if you perform the rituals, belief and understanding will eventually follow. More perfectly translated, it means *we will do, and we will hear*. The writing comes first. The poems themselves are always more intuitive than I am, and bring me closer to others, to understanding, to the inanimate, the infinite, the ineffable. The poems are a listening, an eavesdropping. The poems open their arms to the world, and say *yes* to all encounters.

We spend most of our lives in un-beautiful, banal places, which makes it inevitable that meaningful events will happen in quotidian landscapes and generic spaces, in our cars or standing in line or on public transportation. I live in a semi-rural town where most of us drive everywhere. That means that the places where I meet friends and neighbors—and where I witness the interactions of others—are most often commercial spaces: the checkout line at Walmart, Kroger's deli counter, the pediatrician's waiting room, the gas pumps at Sheetz. In a 1999 interview in the *Literary Review*, poet David Trinidad says this about the use of pop culture in poems: "I suppose there's still, in some quarters, this attitude that poetry has to be above all that, that it has to be this serious, highbrow thing, that the rest is passing garbage and won't last. But it doesn't feel like that for me."

Everyday objects in my poems are both a result of documentation, and a conscious decision on my part. I resist the impetus to iron out brand names, or the detritus of everyday life, because the truth is that life happens at the 7-Eleven near the Slurpee machine, or at the Bank of America ATM. Who decided there's no room in a poem for a bag of Funyuns or a Facebook status update? There is beauty and heartache at the CVS, and the Waffle House—of that, I am absolutely certain.

If this is a manifesto, it's a doubtful one—a what do *you* think manifesto. I seldom trust my intellect. I feel caught, often, between language and emotion and experience. My poems, when I get out of my own way, are generally smarter and braver than I am, built from my experiences and perceptions and connections to the world, and the ways in which my female body moves through it at any given moment.

The personal is always political, and female desire and female bodies are worth writing (and reading) about. I am a poet, a mother, a teacher, a daughter, a partner, and many other things. My body is shifty, but it doesn't always belong wholly to me. My experiences are shifty, but they usually don't belong only to me. My poems are shifty, but they are completely of me, from me, by me—a push-pin on a map, an anchor-drop for the night.

Works Cited

Nemy, Enid. "Lauren Bacall, 89, Dies; in a Bygone Hollywood, She Purred Every Word." *New York Times*, 13 August 2014, p. A1.

Marranca, Richard and Vasiliki Koros. "Pop Culture and Poetry: An Interview with David Trinidad." *The Literary Review*, vol. 42, no. 2, 1999, p. 323.

Erika Meitner

Swift Trucks

This place has views

of black cows, heads bent,
some galloping across a field.

That's from the left side.

To the right, there's the runaway
truck ramp on I-85, rutted

and eschewing abandon.

What isn't stuck somewhere
godforsaken? Only

one of these statements

is true and you get to pick:
he wants to have a word

with us or I can't pay

for gas no more. O Country
View Motel. I press

the shutter release and say

yes to the sound of your
(captured) face, to fists

made of facts, to whatever

doesn't pay the rent but
means well anyway.

This is not the poem

in which someone invented
the term hypnotism.

In which you say yes

to what you see—yes,
we must get it seen to.

Only one of these

statements are true:
your face carries

a certain strangeness

that does not surface
much or your photos

(when threaded together

like jewels) bear every
message you were excited by

when the world spoke to us.

When the world spoke to you
it said stay. It said fragmentary.

Erika Meitner

It touched your face, your

beleaguered tender important face
and said this and this and this.

Continuation

And the neighbor's daughter shows my son
the way her father let her hold his gun,

with bullets in it. She was on Adderall,
and now Ritalin, and they're only in

Kindergarten but my son doesn't much
like her—the way she brags and lies

and tries to destroy the plants or bugs
around our house, which is the bus stop,

so we head out each morning in our
pajamas, clutching coffee mugs, to wait.

The engine of the bus is huffing,
unmistakable, and we can all hear it

before its yellow nose comes around
the bend. The kids climb the high steps

like they're scaling a great peak.
I can see my son fling his body

into a seat; he waves from the window
while Sarah makes her way to her

mandated spot behind the driver,
who waves to us too, then pulls the lever

to shut the doors and heads down Heartwood
Crossing, though the sign says Xing

as the whole name won't fit. This cross-
hatch, this target; X marks the spot

like those yellow and black novelty
signs: Moose Xing, Gator Xing,

Sasquatch Xing. My son loves to watch
the show Finding Bigfoot, where

a research team goes to Rhode Island,
Alaska, New York, to investigate

a recent spike in Squatch sightings.
Each episode is exactly the same,

save for the location: they go out
as a team one night to look for bigfoot,

call for him, and find signs. Next,
they have a town hall meeting

to discuss sightings with residents
who tell stories, which they recreate

using a giant guy named Bobo as a stand-in,
and they always come to the conclusion

that the resident did see a bigfoot—
that bigfoot could definitely live in

_____. We live in blank.
Sarah's mother threw her father out

for keeping a loaded Uzi on the floor
of their garage. When Sarah aims,

with her fingers, at the empty birds' nests
in the eaves of our porch, I wait for her

to say bang, but instead she repeats
it had bullets in it, and there's the bus

wheezing around the bend again,
yellow as a road sign, a daffodil,

a stretch of CAUTION tape.

Orlando Menes
Manifesto

I claim the Baroque as my poetics, specifically the Neo-Baroque, also called Ultra-Baroque, its provenance Latin American, more accurately Caribbean (i.e., *Barroco*, its trilled *r* a call to carnivalesque revolutions, to apocalyptic rumbas), my metaphors dense, fecund as the jungle *manigua*, my ideas effusively abstract, gorgeously convoluted as the roots of the ficus, the banyan, the strangler fig, every utterance labored to beauty, though not that round, smooth pearl of Classical perfection, but more the gnarled, grotesque, gargantuan nacre of our fallen world. My forefathers are Alejo Carpentier, José Lezama Lima, Severo Sarduy, perhaps Hart Crane and Wallace Stevens for their efflorescent imaginations, transmutative tropes—yes, yes, even Anglos can dance deliriously if tropicalized in the mind. My lines are impacted, congested, an excess of rhythm and motion, a surfeit of cross-cultural motifs, myriad marvelous syncretisms and heretical permutations—*mestizaje* on steroids (Oh, so shamelessly extravagant). Carpentier writes, ". . . all symbiosis, all hybridity, engenders the Baroque." My raison d'etre as a poet (a kind of vatic calling) is to erase all demarcations of culture and religion, to trouble canons of propriety, to insist that words belong to no nation, to no race, and thus amenable to heteroglossic agglomerations, to many-tongued mélanges, tempestuous and unruly, prone to wild divinations, that tribalistic cult of the sacred.

Works Cited

Carpentier, Alejo. "The Baroque and the Marvelous Real." *Magical Realism: Theory, History, Community,* edited by Lois Parkinson Zamora and Wendy B. Faris, Duke UP, 1995, p. 100.

Doña Flora's Hothouse

The Sargasso Sea in cyclone
season, a flotilla of blessèd corpses
drifting in equatorial currents,
their shaved heads crowned with laurel
to repel lightning, sargassum fronds
swathing both neck and limb.

Tiny crabs burrow ears
oozing cerumen, pipefish slither
into sutured wounds that coffer
bones of African St. Barbara.

In the tropics the blessèd are incorruptible,
whether Goa, Malabo, or Hispaniola.
Landfall at Doña Flora's island
(longitude of Gonave and Barbuda),
green thumb hermit who cultivates

their bodies in a hothouse by the sea.
Sheared parts fructify in African soil
from Ilé-Ifé, guano of *Caná-Caná*
vulture that flies to heaven carrying
missives, prayer beads and pits.

Swinging her calabash censer,
Doña Flora fumigates with sarsaparilla
entrails of tamarind, soursop kidneys,
banana toes; a *zunzuncito* hummingbird
flies out her ear to sip balsam tears.

Suspended amid laelia orchids
mulatto cherubs trumpet *sones*
from Oriente, Doña Flora rattles
her maraca to sprinkle aguardiente
on guava bladders, uteri of red
papaya, mango hearts. By white

mangroves a shanty of lignum vitae,
dried thatching, barnacled crosses.
All Soul's Day and Doña Flora enters
with her animals, laying overripe fruits

on whitest linen. Iguanas chew
sweet-acid tamarind, a *jutía* rat
nibbles guava, *Caná-Caná* rips papaya—
seeds bursting out—as Doña Flora skins

a mango, bruised with machete,
lifts the bleeding fruit to bands
of amber light, sweet flesh dissolving
in her mouth, its bare stone returned to sea.

Cenobites

Heaven is bone dust and iodine clouds.
Alluvial marrow, gallstone cays.
Cenobites dredge mangrove catacombs,
Then lathe in the sun finger-bone amulets,
Scrimshaw doxologies of femur & tibia.
On the leeward side they plow high bluffs—
Tartar, calculus—sowing tobacco seeds
That thrive in the urate squalls of Lent.
Cenobites canoe to Santiago's islands—
Rocky calvaria—where they cast sisal nets
For fetuses, embryos, even zygotes that escape
Limbo's still waters, & preserved in gourd
Reliquaries the unborn sway from rood
Trees of black mampoo & Guiana rapanea.
As cherubs spawn in lagoons of rheum
& choirs susurrate litanies beneath a rain
Of bile, breakers strew bodies martyred
In fontal seas, every blessèd nose, colon,
Kidney, uterus, cochlea stewed in conch
Pixes for Easter's callaloo, & in their shrine
Of lignum vitae, under a mercuric moon,
The fattened cenobites rhumba la mea culpa.

Susan Laughter Meyers
Manifesto
Willing to Fetch the Water

I.

The secret to writing a poem is to write. The secret to writing a good poem
is to revise. And to read good poems. (These are not secrets.)

Read, write, and—Beckett nailed it—fail. Often. With great energy.
With no regard for outside opinion. And then? *Fail better,* he said.

The poem is not posing or pandering for sighs. Nor is it trying to look
like itself in a former state. It has nothing to do with taxidermy.

~

Once, I would sit on the floor at a typewriter and retype a poem—whole—
draft by draft. That's how revisions arrived, consonant by vowel.

The key would strike, say, the letter *b* on white paper. A revelation—
each word composing itself before me. My task: be still, keep watch.

To retype a poem was to blindly breeze by a line that, draft after draft,
gave me a sinking feeling—and to see, finally, its brokenness.

~

When I'm smart I pay attention to how I feel inside, writing the lines
of a poem and reading them aloud. On good days I listen to my gut.

To title a poem is to put a slant on it, not to pin it down but to let it
fly.
Not to label it but to give it a face. And a name. A life.

A good poem opening is, perhaps, green or yellow or blue—not gray.
However—with the right diction, syntax, voice—the ending could be
gray.

~

A poem that starts out as a sliver, or even a corner of a sliver, may
end up
finding its way into the complications of war, love, death.

Though writing blindly, I'm looking for the odd—for the self.
For the oddness within myself? Yes. I want to shake myself from
dull habit.

Take risks, I hear. It's easy to pull back from the outrageous
and the illogical—but first there must be that wild leap to pull back
from.

~

At the poem's start the reader is stranger; by the end, companion. At
first
what the poet hopes for is curiosity; by the end, empathy—trust.

A poem that doesn't get written evaporates in the air. Someone else
will pluck it. That's what I heard Carolyn Forché say, and I believe it.

One poem leads to the next the way the memory of one dream leads,
day to day, to another. To plant a fern is to turn the whole woods
green.

~

Every line in the poem plays its own part, yes? Shouldn't each be
alive
and willing to fetch the water or, failing that, to tumble downhill?

Every poem in a manuscript needs at least one friend. Two friends,
and a pattern is established. The reader starts nodding with
recognition.

Every poet needs rules. Rules to follow, rules to break. Even the ones
you don't believe give you a tightrope to inch along—or leap from.

2.

For the visual artist there's negative space; for the poet, silence.
A foil for sound. Point, counterpoint: the uttered, the unutterable.

Silence is more than absence. Yesterday the wind shook the leaves
from the trees; today I look at the bare limbs. Is that a rustling I
hear?

~

How to be silent? White space, punctuation, elliptical syntax, the
breath,
the unspoken—each, in its own way, halts the river of sound.

Implication casts its net beyond the poem's words. Early on as a poet
I fell in love with the resonance, the ripple effect, of implication.

~

Silence in a poem is more than a matter of craft, just as being silent
for an hour in my day is more than a matter of keeping my mouth
shut.

Here's the thing: the motor won't cut off. I take it to bed, but it never
runs down. An owl sits in a tree in the back woods, listening.

~

How do I know the owl is there? Because I know. Blue says, sitting
in his recliner when it's dark out, he can feel when the possum
comes.

A poem without silence? Imagine birdsong turned to chatter.
Imagine
a drone of ceaseless notes. The uncurbed loneliness of all that
sound.

~

As reader, I want room to take the words in. Like a bell's tongue,
I want to swing against the poem's walls to sound out the song of it.

Pinpricks of silence let the light in—or the dark. Without warning,
they open up spaces for the unknown. No wonder silence scares us
so.

~

Like writing an erasure poem, to revise toward spareness is to court
silence.
You're left with the poem, plus the ghost words beneath.

Some days I sit on the grass and close my eyes to pretend it's summer.
I can't hear the gossip of gnats circling the hour's long season.

Susan Laughter Meyers

The Tilt That Stumbles Me

I'm driving down the road, by my side a sack
of camellia blossoms and a bee.
The blossoms, their petals silky coins
of pink and red, are stacked and staggered,
some fluted at the edges, some specked with gold.
Beauty heaped in disarray,
though the wrinkled sack lacks all signs of it.
I'm driving down the road with a sack of beauty,
which, I can tell by the buzzing and tapping,
is an ill fit for the bee.
When I pick camellias, I know to hold the blossoms
upside down to free the bees
that may have tunneled deep.
Sometimes the bee does not emerge.
You must learn to look at the world upside down,
the preacher said at Phil's funeral—
the preacher said this clearly, despite his stutter—
the world that will never be the same,
the tilt that stumbles me.
At the light I roll the window down
and open the sack, shaking it and imagining
a kiss of bitterness, and then another, stinging
and singing in circles at my head.
My forehead and nape, the softest
spot on my wrist—they crawl with the song.
But the bee does not emerge.
When the light turns green,
I bear right at Cosgrove—marsh, palmettos,
this sack of beauty. I hear the tapping again,
and again, each time fainter, until no more.

You Offer Apology

but I to you of a white goat
say nothing till barbed

by the fence
that defines this withering.

No climb can snatch
what rises beyond reach.

You I forgive,
sorry or not.

Bearded by what falsehood,
nudged by whose hunger

under
which bridge?

Don't answer that. All I ask
is a creek bed of stones.

The first line is from *If Not, Winter: Fragments of Sappho*, translated by Anne Carson.

Jennifer Militello
The Incongruence Manifesto

A poem should be raw in order to be real. It should place seemingly incongruent items or ideas or images together so that each may be re-seen, so that they can stay with the reader, impale the reader, convert the reader's religion for good. Not just a shiver and a quickening of the heart, but a response that mimics a shift in the physicality of the body and the structure of the brain. A shift in perception, and so reality itself. As happens when an emotion is sealed inside the corpuscles of the frontal lobe. As happens when a memory is made.

I work by the art of context, by positioning for reinvention.

I want my poems buckshot. I want my poems resonant. I want my poems damaged/ing and fierce. A thorn or itch. I want my poems finding their homes beneath the skin.

I want each poem to dream feverishly in its little hive. To wail with its body as well as its bow.

I want a poem to recreate the grand interior labyrinth with an alive, vital order of impressions and refrains. I assemble this entity, the poem, as half object and half animal, so that it may worm into the reader like a parasite and feed her and keep her starving at once. I want to become a carpenter of language, a woodcarver of words, to step carefully among the energy of voice, the music, the breath, the resonance of the exact and spectacular in order to fashion poems imposing and bleak.

I imagine resonance to be a poem's most important tool. The music is there, the image is there, but the between-frequencies of each are what impart a poem its strength.

A poem is the translation, the re-creation, of an emotional truth. When frameworks are skewed, when metaphors are stretched. It must reach beyond the intellect, to the instinct. Our minds respond to meaning, but our hearts respond to sound.

A poem should be tangible, should partner the concrete and abstract. It should capture the complexity of all that happens because we exist. It should take perspective and sweep it into an undertow and sound wave and sail.

A poem should say what cannot be said.

It should birthplace and magnify, fluctuate and confess.

It should allow us to warm our hands at the fire of the world.

Jennifer Militello

A Dictionary of Preserving the Hydrangea's Bloom

First, soften its thousand grand catastrophes of smoke,
small-fisted exotics, unaware of death. Startle the petals'
parchment paper, all in grays beneath the flesh,

scents that have been pinched and rounded, planted down
the hurricane loam, equal parts peat, leaf mold, senile
elegies, lime-free grit. At the center of the hand,

a map for each is pinned. Gestation weeps
more acidity for each deciduous bruise, suggesting
understanding beyond the human crush. Bend

the panicle until it splits, glitters, lords over
the grasp of the stem's relenting vine. Splinter the iris's
dimness, a fine gauze between contrasting eyes. Flay

of the seedless, swimless flutter, lord of the smolder,
the yellow sky's mouths. The last sad vendor
of the intricate's decline. Cover flat with glass and wait.

Architecture: the last occupants, sorrows that are picked,
with fertile or perfect florets, bottles containing poison,
notched, so as to be detected in the dark, by touch.

A Dictionary of Mechanics, Memory, and Skin in the Voice of Marian Parker

The world is a wind I thought I heard just before
I heard nothing. The world is what the pulse of me
whispered just before it stalled. A lullaby
I drugged myself with while my slit throat emptied.

If I had risen the casual distance,
if I had run, if I had resisted like metal
not fired enough—but I can end if one man
asks it of me. Already my sewn eyes

are widows, delicate and desolate, a sabotage
in wails. Every direction in me is south. Every
sleep the deception of sleeping. Every corrosion
another part drought. I prefer to fail. I prefer

to be in pieces. No one expects from me now.
No mourning the model specimen, little Marian,
for what she was. The thin room of my animal's
whimper keeps night from the garden.

My limbs have their own dementia, decomposing
like a bloom. Fathers do not hesitate to collect
my rough bones. I will build a womb bathtub-cold
and be born, white as its porcelain, prone. I will

grow old in the minutes it takes to be dismembered:
one suture for each of my antiseptic mouths.
Tattered is how I began. It pleases me to rest among
the lilies though their bulbs long ago burned out.

Tyler Mills
Manifesto // 22 Dictums // On Balance in the Making of What Escapes Us, i.e., The Poem

1. In another city or town, or in your city or town, people do not have money to eat.
2. In another city or town, or in your city or town, people walk away from where they sleep worried they will be attacked.
3. Poetry cannot feed the person who does not have money to eat.
4. Poetry cannot protect the people who walk away from where they sleep worried they will be attacked.
5. The poet knows these things.

~

6. The poem is a repository: as memory, it should not promise stability.
7. The poem is a repository: as artifact, its language has been torn from experience.
8. The poem is a repository: what it holds is dangerous. What it holds, it holds forever.
9. The poem is not the thing that makes you who you are.

~

10. The poem is a thing made as if by you. The as if? That is the
speaker.

~

11. The speaker addresses a "you" always elsewhere: almost
there. Sometimes this you is the self. Sometimes this you is
the reader.

~

12. The poet should not treat the reader like a consumer.
13. The poem is not to be consumed.
14. The poet should think of the reader as someone who has
decided to walk next to the poet for a time and listen.
15. This listening should not be taken for granted.
16. This listening is not necessary.
17. This listening is rare.

~

18. The poem should scare you, the maker.
19. This scaring is not gratuitous: it comes from a truth.
20. Though its language has been torn from experience, the
poem still promises it.

~

21. Everything is at stake in this promise that a poem makes.
22. This promise is where the poet almost loses the self.

Lesson

Flames ice the grass. Nests of hornets
murmur in the smoke. Clay steams.
Horses snorting ash pass barebacked.
It is not enough to want to leave—
consider the tapestry knotted near the hearth,
the pots and pots of boiled lentils.

All of the nights breathing in that one place,
the dark room where dinner spices hang
above the face the way wind sucks in
through an open window. Lot fed the visiting angels
bread his wife flattened on a stone,
palm on stone, as the men of the city circled.

The men of the city want to fuck the angels.
Screaming horses pass Lot's wife as she climbs
the hill from the Valley of the Salt Sea—
the tents below lit up like blown glass.
All those nights breathing in that one dark room,
remembering: blood on the thighs, wet as tongued

saliva, blood staining the skin—
do not enter. Do not enter. On the hill,
Lot's wife heard her past self's
hair catching fire in the city.
This story is supposed to be a lesson,
someone could remind me. You should not

look for your past self: naked
below, below. Go back.

Get the woman out. The men want
to fuck the angels. A sheep's on fire now,
running. Turn back and get the woman
out of the room. Another horse passes.

Ash, the stairs must be ash now,
and empty. The snapping wood ribs of the room.
The cellophane lens heat casts.
The woman. There won't be any woman
in the wrong bed. She'll get out
so there won't be any woman on a hill.

There won't be any city burning behind,
hot on the back of her thighs. The sweat.
There won't—be any anyone—turn back, watch.

Cyclops

All perspective is is a dot
you can plan on any page
and then draw solid cubes so a house

can hover above crayon spikes of grass.
I am afraid. I have seen sheep puff
like dandelions,

some spotting blue as though thumbs
pushed ink on their backs.
Farmers spray dye on the rams

so after rutting with ewes,
the used ones are marked.
The more a thing is investigated,

the more it burns. Light on paper.
A museum displays these photographs:
Paganini's ghost wearing a devil mask

pushing down on his violin,
and others, a serious girl,
hair parting her skull in half.

People show others how no one *is*
still there—turning a cold doorknob.
And how the more a thing is probed,

the more it burns. O it burns.

Jacqueline Osherow
Opportunism
A Manifesto (With Apologies to Coleridge and Kubla Khan)

Let's say I was reading late into the night a compendium of manifestos and defenses: how a poem must be "better than any movies," provide "a medicine of cherries," how I myself—albeit with no acknowledgement—am in fact legislating the world. Let's say I had trouble sleeping (anxious, perhaps, about this job of global legislation) and took an *anodyne*. In the resulting deep sleep, I saw a scroll unrolling before me the words of an exquisite manifesto and *on awakening* had *a distinct recollection of the whole*. *Unfortunately*, before I could write it down, I was *called out by a person on business from Porlock* and by the time I returned, my manifesto had left my head except for *a vague and dim recollection*.

All I remember is something about the perfect blankness of a page, how a poem must rise to its occasion, and from there press on in incongruent directions, reveling in its own impossibility, flaunting it, wielding it, defying it.

That's it. Now I'm on my own.

And the truth is there's very little I can say. If I try to establish some guidelines, some rules or parameters, some genius will come along with a genius poem and instantly conclusively discredit them. For example, I'm inclined to suggest—given the uncharted territory—that if you're not lost it's probably not a poem. But then I think of Byron, who was never lost in his life. Wherever he felt like being was a poem.

Perhaps I should put that in my manifesto? To find the poem wherever I might be, to say, *here I am! where's my poem?*

And I might as well add something about redefining words, willing them to mean what you need them to mean: reconfiguring proportion (the tiny enormous, the gargantuan minute); proving both a dictum and its opposite; flouting mathematics with an ever-expanding whole vastly greater than its disappearing parts.

Of course, as I describe it, it's undoable. Still, one might as well devise a plan. Mine would begin humbly, with the world as it presents itself, at least as I perceive it, remember it. From such a starting place, my poem would be forced to travel, have the chance to gather momentum for propulsion.

Sometimes it seems to me received forms are the ideal catapults and slingshots. That's what I feel as reader when a confluence of words rearranges the universe and also rhymes. As a poet, I find in forms sonic roadmaps, clues in a cryptic, acoustic treasure hunt—go to this sound, which leads to that sound—a way of making the impossible seem less daunting.

At the same time, forms create a kind of glue, or in the case of terza rima, centripetal force, holding the sprawling contents tight inside a poem's whirling bucket, when by rights they should fly apart. Terza rima's like a Tibetan monk who can sing two notes at once: both lyric and discursive at the same time. Quatrains, on the other hand, enforce restraint, as do certain kinds of rhyming couplets. Villanelles make poems of obsessions.

Still, each is just a way of getting somewhere—a route, a mode of transport. I don't experience form as destination. I like to say I'm not a formalist, but an opportunist, using whatever I think—in a given circumstance—will get me nearest to where I want to go: a place I doubt I've ever been. Still form often gives me at least the illusion of approach, or, on other occasions, a series of expectations against which my poem might explode.

Free verse is, for me, the most demanding and austere of forms; writing in it feels like heading down a washed-out dirt road in one of those gigantic fifties Cadillacs. But sometimes a person has to try to get where she needs to get; sometimes all she has is her uncle's car.

So what do I do now, having backed myself into this corner? I might as well come clean; I'm not Coleridge. (*Those sunny domes! Those caves of ice!)* What poem of mine could accompany this manifesto? How could it do anything but flounder?

On the other hand, what choice do I have? Exhilarating as the blank page is, I'm not content to leave it blank. And to intrude upon that blankness is to trespass on possibility, make another sucker's bargain with the doable. But still, we have evidence. Poems happen. There are words—I've seen them with my own eyes—that, even as they delimit, serve as openings, breaking down the very boundaries they create. If only *I* could *revive within* me *that symphony and song*! Or at least an echo, a variation. . . . *So that all who heard shall see them there.* . . . It's maddening stuff, *the milk of paradise.* My manifesto: *Beware! Beware!*

Poem for Jenne

Larkspur and delphinium, wild and tame
transcriptions of the same essential idiom
(as lullaby, corralled, is requiem,
a sigh, bound and gagged, a lyric poem).

Earth's trying to remake herself with stars,
her own inky domain of skyey colors.
She wants everything. It won't be hers.

Her starry flowers, heedless of safeguards,
will launch their blue and purple rockets heavenwards
and leave her to her dusty browns and reds,
her brief sky shattered, just as words—

the good ones, anyway—will quit this page
before I ever pay this garden homage
or name the pain I'm trying to assuage.

Nonetheless, these clusters *are* in flower
if only for an instant, as they were
a year ago, when Jenne (this poem's for her),
knowing how I love them, put them here

to make the way around my house less bitter.
My next-door neighbor, she'd watched things shatter
and so came by to plant and tend and water

and whatever else it is that gardeners do.
And I remember catching a dim glimpse, as if through
an impossible tunnel—*what's all that blue?*—
and thinking, as one thinks of something wholly out of view,

how lovely it would be to lay my eyes on them,
though they were there, waiting, each time I came home:
larkspur out the back, out front delphinium

(the cultivated version for the public eye,
its wild incarnation just for me . . .)
and once or twice I did suspect that beauty
and kindliness had aimed themselves my way

but each was such a difficult abstraction,
at best unverifiable, uncertain,
a meteor I wasn't sure I'd seen.

I, who'd been so lucky up to then,
was utterly astonished by what pain—
in its purest form—can make out of a person.
It was (such things exist) a brutal season

and one that's not entirely departed
though time has passed; flowers, twice, have sprouted.
The earth will be, twice over, broken-hearted,

which means, at least, according to King David,
in his most unnerving psalm, closer to God.
Me? I'd leave some distance if I could
though it would be untrue to say no good

has come from any of this. See? out my window
the earth again has sheathed herself in indigo;
this may be the time she makes it through:

her sapphire daggers, bursting their scabbards,
carve frantic constellations: elfin songbirds
vehement with blue and purple chords;
earth's reaching for her heavens, I for words

or any chink of rapture I can claim.
Delphinium. Larkspur. Larkspur. Delphinium.
Let me claim you as you climb and climb.

White on White

after Kasimir Malevich

It's the sort of painting I could never stand—
a white square askew on a white background—

one more aesthetic incarnation
of that swindled emperor, naked again,

preening in his nonexistent clothes;
I'd lived in Florence—where painting breathes—

seen how inanimate materials
(gold beaten to dust, crushed-up jewels

mixed for rich and lasting color with albumen)
could be converted into pure emotion,

how master after master after master
had willed a chapel wall of fresh wet plaster

to make the ephemeral hold still
alongside the godly, the impalpable.

Why would you paint a white square askew
on a white background when you could go

anywhere at all, encompass anything?
If the world failed us, at least a painting

might offer us its aggregate of rapture.
I had a stake in this, longed to capture

a bit of it myself (though my materials
would be more modest, words instead of jewels)

or at least exhaust myself in the attempt;
I was a seasoned dreamer and I dreamt,

which sustained me for quite a number of years.
But even the most stubborn of dreamers

is forced to notice, sooner or later,
that the world understands itself without her

albeit flattering intrusion
and it's a meager place once illusion

in all its glory is exposed as sham.
Besides, I've squandered poem after poem.

Just think of all the treasure I've left stranded,
uncultivated, the unattended

but manifest allegiances in things,
how a presence, of its own accord, sings

right within my own field of vision
and I always fail to take it down:

the year the snow came late and the mountain
was suddenly a tour-de-force of ermine

white on the golden residue of aspens
(it's the winter slant of light that determines

the color of their fur and not the snow)
or a June hike—what?—fifteen years ago,

the mountainside a visual haiku:
five mountain goats on the last patch of snow

and I would leave them there, forgotten.
That is, until, by accident I wandered in-

To the wrong room at MOMA, turned around
to a white square askew on a white background

and there were my mountain goats on snow.
Kasimir Malevich had seen them too,

how white craves white, how what's askew
yearns for some congenial milieu

where it can lose itself, disappear.
Those stunning ermine that snowless year

were neon on the gold leaves' makeshift carpets,
thrilling to witness, but ideal targets

for even the most dull-eyed predator.
Better to secure a sound white square

however unremarkable, unsubtle.
A person has to settle for what's possible.

A white square on a white background, askew.
Five mountain goats on the last patch of snow.

Emilia Phillips
"X: A Manifesto of Poetics"

When that burning bush of my brain starts proclaiming law, I make
a break back down the mountain. Perhaps it's because I don't want
poetry to accomplish only one effect—on me, my readers. I don't want
poetry for poetry's sake, don't want to make it into a key that fits only
one lock. I love poetry—*want* poetry—for its implications in other areas
of my life. I want poems that comfort, that appeal to a death-wish
undercurrent; that play to my strengths, and my weakness; that make
me horny, that remove me from my body; that empathize, and debate;
that stimulate my salivary glands like baking bread; that indulge my
obsessions; that purge me, and that burden me. If I start writing
knowing which of these outcomes I'm writing toward, it will seem
redundant and therefore dull, like seeing too many photos of Stone-
henge before one gets there. I always want to arrive in poems, not
return. Even if that sometimes means missing the mark.

(Writing my poetic manifesto is a bit like chalking an outline before
there's a body; every time I outline what I value, what I adhere to in
my writing, those things change.)

Reading Ovid at the Plastic Surgeon's

I scarcely dared to look
to see what it was I was.

No one else with a book, the slick
weeklies gossip amongst

themselves on the side
tables as the ticker rolls the Dow

Jones *down down down* under
a profile of the marathon

bombers (the older, a boxer). Jove
argues for the removal of a race

of peoples that do not please
him: *What is past*

remedy calls for the surgeon's
knife. He will take a hunk of my

cheek (cancer) and though I can't
see mid-procedure, I imagine

the site as an apricot, bitten.
This, a survival mechanism—

romanticism. David says,
If you're out

in public and you don't want anyone
to talk to you, bring a book

of poetry. Even as I enter the confidence
of the room, I avoid my

reflection in the window, for there,
most of all, I see myself as only I can,

as only the eye will have me—
as light, as light alone.

Aubade

Sometimes we say to one
    a goodbye
      meant for another. Morning
and the meperidine dream
        breaks to shaking. My husband

guides me by his hands
    on my
    hips like a window-
dresser wheeling a mannequin
        into sunlight, toward its reflection. I dreamt

of being, like fruit,
    faceless.
    The surgeon insists it's
the swelling. He must've learned
        to stitch on the flesh of an

orange, unless this idea is an ambrosia
    the gods pretend
    to eat so that when we steal,
we steal pathetically.
        The bath reminds me

of a lover. The meperidine
    guides me by its
    hands on
the glass. He holds my head as if a baby's
        and tilts me back. I dreamed of being faceless

like morning. The bath reminds me
of a window. The dream—
it breaks like a stitch. . . .
Sometimes we say to one the goodbye
another meant.

Kevin Prufer
A Manifesto

1. A complaint

Here's what I learned in school about reading poems: Poems are
different from stories or movies. The former entertain us with a fic-
tional narrative while the latter present us with super-condensed lan-
guage. Within that language lies a tangle of metaphor, simile, allegory,
and symbol wrapped in a skin of metrics. I was taught that reading a
poem involved mostly *decoding*, figuring out which nouns were symbols
and which were parts of metaphors. Did the poem engage in strange
fits of music? What did that mean? Could I make an argument for the
symbolic meaning of, say, water? Or light? Or a pigeon?

If I read a poem closely enough, I learned, I could solve the whole
thing and, in so doing, come to an understanding, which I learned to
call an *interpretation*.

It took me years to unlearn this, to realize that it's a poor way of
reading poetry—and not just because it's joyless and clinical. If we think
that poets write in a language that must be deciphered, then we make
poetry appealing only to fans of crossword puzzles and cryptograms.

Moreover, if we believe poetry is a kind coded language, we also
believe, implicitly, that the primary work of the poet isn't communica-
tion at all. Codes exist to impede communication, not to facilitate it.
If poetry is a kind of code, then the writer and the reader must work
against each other, one acting to conceal and the other acting (if he
cares to!) to break through that concealment.

As an early reader of poetry, I was always at odds with the poet. A poem was that unpleasant conflict embodied on the page.

2. But—

I believe that almost all great poems are difficult. Their difficulty, however, has nothing to do with code breaking. Or, if a little decipherment is necessary, that's just part of how the poem is trying to communicate.

Emily Dickinson is a difficult poet because the questions she asks in her poems are difficult to answer. *Is there a God?* she asks. She doesn't know. Tough question. *What happens after you die?* Again, hard to know. Like all of us, Dickinson wrestles with the big truths. Like the thoughtful among us, she doesn't know the answers. She feels one way, and *wants* to feel another. Part of her believes simultaneously conflicting things about the nature of the divine and a third part is pretty sure the concept is empty. Her poems are urgently trying to communicate this double- or triple-minded thinking to us and, truly, she's being as clear as her complex subjects will allow. Still, the poems are not easy to read. They require work on the part of the reader. Difficult questions, difficult answers.

Call it ambivalence—thinking and feeling in multiple, sometimes contradictory directions. Poetry is an art form uniquely suited to expressing the workings of a complex mind in motion, a mind that struggles with difficult questions.

3. Some History—

The defining quality of sentimental poetry isn't an overabundance of emotion, nor is it inappropriate emotion. Lots of sentimental poetry has a *proper* amount and quality of emotion (if emotion, tossed into a poem, can be measured and found proper and fitting). Sentimental poetry, I've decided, reduces what ought to be complex feelings and thoughts to simplistic ones.

We are suspicious of sentimental language because it is not just icky, but also dangerous. Sentimental language provides us with images of laughing, happy slaves. It praises the feminine in ways that close out women's real lives and desires. Wrapped in the goo of nationalism, it tells young people to go off to battle, to die for flag and country. Sure, sentimental language makes us giggle, but it is to be feared. It has allowed us to ruin lives. It's ruined lives.

4. A Void

I once thought that it was uncool to write about powerful feelings because that was sentimental. My poems were going to be hard little gems of irony, they were going to announce themselves with a startling interplay of competing surface textures. Pastiche, intertextuality, self-referentiality, pop culture—a lovely glittering surface concealing nothing, because the truth I was after was that there is no truth to speak of. What was I thinking? Was this the ultimate simplification of emotion and thought, creating in its place a void? Was this as sentimental as I could possibly be?

5. Doublethought

I believe the work of the poet is, at its core, a kind of communication. The poet whispers into the ear of the reader or she announces her truths through a megaphone to a crowd of onlookers. Or, just as often, she communicates with the reader telepathically, the reader observing in her work the poet's mind in motion, hesitating, thinking, turning back on itself, rethinking. It's all communication.

More than any other art form, poetry is able to enact double-mindedness and ambivalence. Poets have at their fingertips all the tools of the writer of prose and much more. The music of the poetic line communicates a truth counter to the words contained in that line. The white space between stanzas expresses unarticulated thoughts, thoughts that may (or may not) be articulated in the next stanza. The rhymed word recalls or undercuts the word it rhymes with. With these and so much more, the poem emerges in its contradictions, questions, shades of competing meanings.

We communicate to each other, and the not-yet-born, the ways our minds work, how our feelings intersect with our thoughts.

6. Political

The television tells me what to believe. So does the newspaper and the computer. I look up to see banner headlines rolling along the lower part of the screen, a ticker-tape of single-mindedness. There are too many people shouting at me about how I ought to behave politically, who want my support. Some have good intentions and some, I believe, have evil ones. The entire production—the clamor of competing voices and sound bites—is probably necessary, though usually unpleasant to listen to.

But poetry doesn't engage with politics that way. Poetry lives in a political world, but probably isn't going to ask for your vote. Good poems aren't single-minded enough to shill; they aren't *simple* enough. Alive in contradictions and difficulty, they might abhor injustice, but tell us about it complexly, recognizing an emotionally fraught terrain for what it is, looking forward to what might be with, perhaps, equal parts hope and despair. Although a poem might have a conscience, it probably hasn't figured out the answer to the question it wrestles with. Not completely, anyway.

It may be that the poem recognizes that many-mindedness is an antidote to political simplicity. And by communicating that ambivalence, the poem makes us more human, more capable of political empathy and complexity.

If my poems are political—and these days they are—I want them to engage in complex political thinking. I want them to be part of a much larger conversation from which come no clear answers, but a deepening understanding about the nature of the questions and why they are important and human and necessary. That's what I mean when I say writing a poem is engaging in an act of *communication*. That's what I want to read, too.

Bread and Cake

The black Mercedes
with the Ayn Rand
vanity plate
crashed through
the glass bus stop
and came to rest
among the bakery's
upturned tables.
In the stunned silence,
fat pigeons descended
to the wreckage
and pecked at
the scattered
bread and cake.
The driver slept,
head to the wheel.
The pigeons grew
rich with crumbs.
The broken glass winked.
God grinned.

Kevin Prufer

How He Loved Them

How much the colonel loved his granddaughters
you will never know.
                        Their laughter filled his black Mercedes
the way a flock of starlings might fill a single tree
with song.
            What he'd had to do that day, he'd done
with a troubled heart,
                        but now their laughter overwhelmed him
with such inarticulable love
                        he could hardly
contain it
            and neither could the empathetic little bomb
in the engine,
                which chose that moment
to burst through the hood with self-obliterating joy.

+

And the Mercedes burned in front of the courthouse.

And the black smoke billowed and rose like a heart full of love.

And the colonel rose, too,
                        like burning newspaper
caught in the wind,
                        a scrap of soot, then nothing, then unknowable—

+

You will never know
            what dying is like.

The colonel's granddaughters are still laughing in the backseat,

or they are uncomfortable in the new bodies
the bomb made for them.

Oh, darling, darling, one of them recalled,
you are burning up
                with fever—her mother's cool hand on her forehead,
then the sense of slipping under,
                  into black sleep. *She's asleep now,*
the voice said, turning out the light,
                    closing the door.

+

And in every hand, smartphones made footage
of their bodies,
           the heaps and twists of metal.

The smoke uploaded the wreckage
                  to the screenlike sky
where it goes on burning forever—

You will never know if dying is like that,
the same scenes repeated across a larger mind
                  than yours—

+

Is it like a small girl with a high fever asleep in a dark room
recollected for a moment
                              as the brain closes down?
She's asleep, the voices say, *she is resting.*

(*My fleeting one, my obliterated device, my bit of pixilated
soot.*) Hit *Pause*
                    and the smoke stops: a black pillar
that weighs the wreckage down.
                                        Then *Play*—
how much he loved them,
                              unknowable—

+

What the colonel had done that day
                                        had troubled his heart,
but the sound of his granddaughters' laughter
lifted him high into the air
                              like a scrap of burning paper
blown from the street into the trees.

Immigration

When the wheels came down over Miami
the stowaway in the landing gear,
half frozen and unconscious,
slipped from the wheel wells into blue air.
How amazed he must have been
to wake to that falling sensation
and the rapidly approaching sodium lamps
of the airport parking lot.

The couple that owned the car his body crushed
was astonished at the twist of fate
that brought his life so forcefully into theirs.
Their young son would always remember it,
how just then the cold shadow of another airplane
passed over him, how the bits of jewel-like glass
lay strewn across the asphalt
like the dead man's thoughts.

Joshua Robbins and Jeffrey Schultz
Subscendentalism

Western poetics is, to put it simply, a series of shifts in the concep-
tualization of the mimetic object. The Greeks were not entirely wrong,
but because they based aesthetic judgment on art's ability to repeat back
a deeply hierarchical, stratified, unjust, and utterly brutal society, they
weren't entirely right either. Next, the Judeo-Christian tradition gained
a foothold in the edifice of the Classical as forms and content once
considered too "low" to be given any attention became integrated into
the tradition, but as political systems expanded geographically and
grew more complex and ur-bureaucratic in structure, poetry's concep-
tualization followed suit. With the Industrial Revolution's turn towards
the primacy of technology, the Romantics attempted, against com-
merce's massive assault on the individual, to find meaning in the loss
of nature and self, but their efforts were upended by the end of the
nineteenth century when such a search could no longer continue un-
ironically, which lead to the modern shift toward a deeply ironic rep-
resentation aware of its own core aesthetic contradiction.

Our relatively recent shift into so-called "postmodern" poetry is
really little more than a reification of modernist poetic consciousness:
poetry is superficially aware that it is poetry. Such a limited and curi-
ously ahistorical awareness does reflect back to us an aspect of experi-
ence, but it does nothing and can do nothing to clarify or contextual-
ize and so transform experience.

We argue that poetry ought to rise above our culture of ideological
constriction and its theodicy of evil and idiocy. Poetry must become

un-adumbrated objectivity, aware of itself as art, but also as aesthetic and social history in the broadest possible sense. Silence is not an option. Silence is complicity.

The only way we can achieve this objectivity is through a poetics which attempts to understand not only our individual experience, but everything that has had a hand in making us and our experiences, and in order to avoid falling back into the feedback loop of what is, it must also be a poetics of justice with a commitment to the representation of what is suppressed by the ideological. The present moment requires a poetics of subscendence. The subscendental poem comes from below, from the hidden underbelly of the official version of experience. It seeks a through and a beyond, all the while it is anchored inextricably to the ground on which we stand.

Subscendentalism is fundamentally materialist: in thinking, in critique, in composition. Subscendentalism is an attempt to bring the transcendent down to Earth, and to bring it down to Earth so that its implications can no longer be pushed outside of the bounds of our actual lives, in order that those moments which give life positive meaning might become part of life itself and not taken as a sign of some other thing.

In our subscendence, we are dialectical and materialist metaphysicians, a contradiction in terms that could only find its resolution in that same origination point, that same singularity from which our history, aesthetics, mimesis, physics, and, finally, our everything, burst forth.

Joshua Robbins
Exchange

It begins always with what's soon-gone: a fleeting apparition,
some neurochemical firing deep within the gray matter's

pathology of need. It is why the body of the speculator,
falling now from forged steel and into the open palm

of the churning Missouri below, knows all there is to know of value
and why the blank billboard on the bridge railing above him whispers

the one pragmatic sweet nothing we all long to hear: *available.*
And it is why, too, any allegory of desperation must first

be wrenched from the calloused fists of those-that-don't
before it can be transferred, with deference, into the soft,

expectant hands of those-that-do: brokenness and regret
are worth as much as shattered plate-glass or a brick's weight

landing on the lacquered floor inside the mini-mart as they are
the hunger of the woman who threw it, and all remain meaningless

until demand sets in. But for now, the man falling is still a man
and is yet as meaningless as the sky which remains clear and seems

somehow suddenly permanent, like the way two long-constellated
indigo stars tattooed on the skyless, freckled, inner left thigh

of a woman I'd fallen for, how they return in memory
as if out of the blue. How it is as if pressing my lips to them

now wouldn't cost me everything. As if it would. As if every moment,
even one as insignificant as this, someone standing awash

in gas station fluorescence, diesel stench, has its asking price,
that the gears of common disaster are oiled by the prayers

of those who've lost. The world is falling.
The world is falling and this afternoon one errant key stroke

concealed behind Kansas City cubicle walls sent wholesale
systems of mutual exchange into digital collapse. A single

"fat finger" depresses "B" as in "billion" not "M" as in "million,"
and on Wall Street, DiModica's *Charging Bull*, stuck good

and bleeding out, torques its horns to gore and hurtles headlong
toward the pecuniary abyss. As confession, cries of *Buy* or *Sell*

are meager substitutions for remorse while the Big Board scrolls
and glows ever bluer. As blue as the sky over the river now,

or over gray Manhattan sidewalk in '29, "Black Tuesday,"
when the ruined leapt from window ledges and prayed

in their descent that, for a moment, the sky would be willing
to exchange what they knew they'd done for whatever oblivion

it could offer. But, if confession is worth nothing,
what would it have earned her then, when she told me

she was beaten as a girl by her father? How anything was a motive.
Poor grades, forgotten laundry. And what would it gain me now

to say that only once, and without regret, he let fall
from his hand the electric iron, and then held its hot aluminum

soleplate against his daughter's leg? Because he *had* to. Because
I love you. What wouldn't be a fair wage for what she earned there?

Why not incise her proud flesh with ink where metal burned,
make permanent the pattern of that which losing makes?

Don't deny it: every thing transacts. Always has. Barley for corn
and rock salt for sea—. The first copper ingot's pressed ox hide

for trial-and-error's blistered palms. And now: the express pay's
binary code, its digitized *chirp* for the debit account's swiped plastic

as the pump's electric numerals blink ever closer to zero balance
where the woman behind the register counts down her till. Another
    day

sold for six dollars an hour at the far-flung periphery of single-zoned
Midwestern sprawl. Here, even the most casual manifestations of desire

triggers in each of us a nerveless shiver of want, like the way
condensation's invisible hand ghosts mini-mart cooler glass,

or how capital's high gloss unconscious drifts on an odor
of citrus-scented industrial cleanser and falls like a kiss upon the lips

and cheeks of the bored waiting for her to take their cash.
Above the checkout, the nightly news is stocks, a local suicide,

and beamed-in highlights of uproar overseas. Again, the ritual
exchange: skull crack for the blackjack's stun, the riot shield's

advancing polycarbonate, a jawbone dislodged. In hi-def,
does the coin-like aftertaste which the brain synthesizes

in the instant before consciousness fades and the body drops,
reveal itself as blood, or as something *more* real? If there were

a stench of paraffin, burning rubber, as the helmeted phalanx
closed, would we know it? Above the megaphone's command,

chopper blades *thwomp* the dusty contours of moonlit cobblestone.
Teargas plumes. And now we go on watching

as if value's vanishing point will never fall below
the horizon, as if this exchange should go on forever.

Jeffrey Schultz
Habeas Corpus

in memoriam the once-frozen North

Our collective consciousness does not allow punishment
where it cannot impose blame.
        United States v. Lyons
    —Judge Alvin Benjamin Rubin, dissenting

There is of course the other idea: that the intricate latticework
Of our bodies loosed from us at last will leave us free
To become anything, pure light, perhaps, or wing-beats

In fresh powder beneath some maples locked up in their thin veneer
Of ice. But then as always a sudden gust and the limbs' clacking,
And, as when some insurgent sound crosses over the porous border

Of a dream, the world recrystallizes around us: midday, snow-
Grayed, the wind-chill's sub-zero like a ball-peen to the forehead.
It's cold enough to quiet even the soul's feathery throat-song,

And so it does. Nothing moves and I move through the woods
At the edge of its city with dog, hoping he'll shit his daily shit
Before this reddening flesh numbs entirely. Nothing moves,

But beneath months-thick ice and powder, winter's put up its dead:
Squirrels and sparrows, the wren and the fox, whole families
Of field mice posed as if in the pet store's deep freeze, even,

Here and there, scattered and whole, occasional missing persons.
For now, for guilty, for guiltless, no matter, the world offers neither
Deliverance nor decay, and though we trust in that the thaw

Will come, that someday soon some pond water, water
Still and softly rippled as pre-War window-glass, will again reflect
Its image of the bloodless sky, cut, at intervals, by spring's

First returning vultures, and though the police will then take
A little comfort, as they kick the MOBILE CRIME LAB'S tires
Before rolling it out for the season, that the birds help at least

To ease the legwork, we know no one's, you know, going to be
Set free. The skull's thin as eggshell so far as the beak's thick curve
Is concerned. The raisin of the eye's an easy delicacy.

And so to imagine the future is to imagine the present, but warmer,
But more forthrightly, more honestly violent. And so another day's
Bones picked clean. There is of course the idea's consolation:

For eternal patience, eternal reward, for the meek, the Earth's
Corpse. Instead, a sort of waking sleep, a sort of waking slow;
We rub our eyes, warm the last of yesterday's coffee, stare

As our email loads: surely something must have come, surely
Someone has spirited us that which would make all the difference.
We call to complain that nothing's working because we like

The on-hold music, which is a sound other than our breathing.
We ask the music if we can speak to its supervisor but when we try
To explain it only laughs, *Guiltless! Who do you think you are anyway?*,

Laughs its little soprano sax laugh before it loops back to its loop's
Beginning. The coffee pot runs on mediated coal and drips acids.
The car's topped up with artillery and emits amputees. The idea was

Waking would make things clearer, would startle us as from any night's
Nightmare: these sheets' cold which is not bare concrete floor,
This patch of light the moon has cast not the interrogator's light,

This knocking in our head not some still-indecipherable code
Tapped against an adjacent wall by who knows who, by someone
We can't even begin to imagine, someone stuck here longer

Than even ourselves yet still committed to the idea that finding
A way to speak to each other would help matters, this knocking
None of that but rather something real, here, furnace clank or thief

In the night, something real and something present and not
The dream of what must be held that way until it stops thrashing,
Not the dream of being held that way, but what could be danger

Or else nothing once more, which means we prowl once more
The house, ridiculous in our underwear, ridiculous with a flashlight
Gripped like a truncheon, the floorboards cold somehow as bare

Concrete, the floorboards that croak somehow like vultures who are
Not here, who winter south, scan the Sonoran desert's northern
Edge, its empty water bottles and tire ruts and those nameless

It dries to a sort of jerky, those nameless who labored in vain
To cross it, who had hoped that in crossing, they would be set free.
Nothing's wrong, the house secure, bolts bolted, latches latched.

Somewhere in the distance beyond the kitchen window, downtown
And its bus bench bail bondsman, downtown and its graffiti
Covered wall's Great Writ: *Repent! The End Is Nigh! As always, as always,*

Answers the darkness. But, pre-War? In what will soon enough be
Dawn-light, in this near-light, who can tell if it's blood spread thin
On our hands or else just a healthy, living glow? Outside the idea

Of night and the idea of day seem to have come to a standoff.
No one's calling for negotiations. We know what happens next:
Whether the stars flicker or merely flinch, the sun, whose face

Is a badge, has always been a little trigger happy. And though
The firestorm will consume, soon enough, everything, it seems
For the moment this will go on. As if indefinitely. As if without cause.

Zach Savich
Living Hand Poetics

The only quality I care about in poetry this morning is presence, present attention, presentations of live being that make any moment feel like morning. One finds it at the end of Keats' "This living hand," which offers the poet's still-live palm like a steaming canapé on a cocktail waiter's tray:

> This living hand, now warm and capable
> Of earnest grasping, would, if it were cold
> And in the icy silence of the tomb,
> So haunt thy days and chill thy dreaming nights
> That thou would wish thine own heart dry of blood
> So in my veins red life might stream again,
> And thou be conscience-calm'd—see here it is—
> I hold it towards you.

Forget poetry that doggedly rehearses orthodoxies of sentiment or slippage, of ideas that are just the scars of past experiences, of philosophically minor conceptualizations that are anxious to be theoretically unassailable. Live presence is wholly, immaculately assailable, bringing us to our senses at the slightest breeze, unworried about making more of anything except itself, another moment, keep talking so I can look at you, ask me a question so we can stay together a little longer. Where? Right here, the poems I care about insist.

Yes, *here* is only a word. And nothing stays still. Presence thus travels, rapid and vast, running through us, running us through. It doesn't worry about performing a thesis or establishing a brand, a persona, a self that is more than expectant, receptive, both actively primed and luxurious in its dereliction (as in Walt Whitman's loafing, as in Robert Lowell's "The Lesson," which begins, "No longer to lie in bed reading *Tess of the d'Urbervilles*"). I've been finding it everywhere, with increasingly sophisticated ease. It turns out that the light around me is very trustworthy and new. Here it is in a recent poem by Ralph Angel, which mercifully puts a coffee pot in a living hand:

> The palms are nice.
>> As is the latticework
>
> (is that jasmine?)
>> for your protection.
>
> And next to the bowl of plums
>> a small bronze coffee pot
>
> right where your hand
>> is nearly touching it.
>
> Yes,
>> it's the best spot
>> and exactly where to stop.

"Is that jasmine?", the poem interrupts itself, showing that attention nests, layers, and textures itself, finding each potential synonym for the present instant a distinct term. The poem comes fully to attention. What more can be said? One looks up and blinks. Much as the earliest travel guides were etiquettes on how to see—you weren't given the history of a famed mountain, but advice about how to perceive it—such poems offer ways of seeing.

Such poems believe that, despite voluble, fashionable dogmas, we haven't exhausted language's potential as a sensory organ, an instrument of perception that moves at the speed of tongue, a mechanism of conjuring, which, in what we could call Kenneth Koch's translation of Keats, wants more from even what we currently hold, the hand already in our hand:

Poetry, my enemy!
Why can't you do everything?
Make me young again.
Give me that hand in my hand.

The kind of presence I have in mind—its stunned clarity—may involve description, but without the look-at-me convolutions of prettily pleased word-painters, and it's distinct from projects of transcription, of real-time simulation, such as Georges Perec's approach to landscape in *An Attempt at Exhausting a Place in Paris* or others' absorbing cognitive perambulations. Its New York School patron poet would be James Schuyler, that rapt naturalist of perceptions with hours around and through them, as delicate and complex as tea made from the third steeping:

> tree shadows on
> grass blades and grass
> blade shadows. the air
> fills up with motor
> mower sound. The cat
> walks up the drive
> a dead baby rabbit
> in her maw.

Schuyler's poems move across the scene like a sprinkler's gentle wave; they have a resuscitational effect, keeping their particulars alive, while also emphasizing their ephemerality. Donald Revell, in his luminous book *The Art of Attention* (from which this morning's manifesto takes a fair portion of its idiom and surge) notes, similarly, that reading can be a way of "praying too, asking God to watch over the animal, to prosper the flower, to mend the bird." This kind of life-giving literacy often depends on the evocation of death, and I admit that the more death becomes a part of my life, the more I'm drawn to poetry's orienting liveliness. Keats' poem offers such an evocation, with a rhetorical structure that recalls Shakespeare's presentation of a time of year in which "yellow leaves, or none, or few, do hang" in "Sonnet 73"—he takes away all the leaves, and then restores a few living ones, holding them toward us.

One may wonder how anything, being read, doesn't offer (and require) present attention. Oh, I don't have a problem with an idea that applies to everything, one way or another, and in my own work, aspiring toward Living Hand Poetics, with the definition staying loose, has been formally useful, by which I mean joyful. The poem becomes an act of presence, of sensual presencing, which is a type of pleasure even when it aches; its achievement doesn't depend on adherence to memory or demonstration of a conceit, or passing the proving ground of a form or a concept (that is, of a pose that will be recognized as a form, a concept), or its connection to the approved news cycles of narrow topicality, but rather on coming intently to a live instant, on coming to, which summons less apparent topicality, like a newspaper with a hole in it. One dives, which makes the water deep.

The hand that is living may be your own! Hold it toward me! Hold it toward me again!

Works Cited

Angel, Ralph. *Your Moon*. New Issues, 2014.

Keats, John. *Complete Poems*. Modern Library, 1994.

Koch, Kenneth. *Collected Poems*. Knopf, 2007.

Lowell, Robert. *Collected Poems*. FSG, 2007.

Revell, Donald. *Art of Attention*. Graywolf, 2007.

Schuyler, James. *Collected Poems*. FSG, 1995.

Zach Savich

The Hopelessly Open Gate

I sit on my perfect bench
and disperse with the train crowd

you know these are cherries by the rough bark
also the fruit

you know a tree fell here
by how finely saplings grew

now take a consequential breath
the wedge you cut has all the lemon's juice

nest held by feathers moving in it

my eyes have no color but what they saw

Smaller Balcony

Spraypainting the bicycle

I had higher hopes for the paint it would leave on the grass

*

Then my hangovers just stopped

What do bees know
There's more honey in my mouth

*

I assumed every poem mentioned the sun
(my way of reading)

There was a plow you led around by being there

Coffee is a little kid

*

Anywhere you put it will be eye level

The vase
The one packed in sweaters

*

Leaves that fall so far should have two names

In conclusion, tulips grown enough for school
I'll walk them

*

The chair has a place for your neck if you lean
When will you be back

There's a lemon under that bowl

Martha Silano
Three Choices
A Manifesto

The whole notion of a manifesto—so presumptuous, so hierarchi-
cal. Listen-to-me-and-you'll-surely-succeed-opolis. Yo! I'm the haps;
I've got the goods! All you gotta do is _____. All you need is
_____. You gotta write poems that _____ and _____. And,
if we all who presume to know fill in the blanks, where does that leave
us? I'm asking you because I don't presume to know. I'm asking you:
are you really looking for The Answer from the poets of 2014? What
will the poets of 2014 look like in, say, 3114? If you go back a 1,100
years in the English language, it looks like this:

> Hwaet! We Gar-Dena in geardadum,
> beodcyninga brym gefrunon,
> hu oa aebelingas ellen fremedon
> Oft Scyld Scefing sceabena breatum

That's the first four lines of *Beowulf*, 900 AD. If this manifesto I'm
composing lasts a thousand years, what makes you think it'll be legible?
English is a mongrel, cannibalizing tongue. It morphs like a virus,
snatches and accommodates adventitious genes like antibiotic-resistant
bacteria. Like anthrax. One second it's grooving along, sounding all
Shakespearean—*oh, for a muse of fire!*—the next *reify* and *mansplaining, bromance*
and *selfies*.

That said, who can resist the request to spell out The Way in hot
pink flashing neon, to don the tiara, profess the path toward the lumi-
nescent end of the lightning bug? I'm all geared up to share! I have

wisdom to impart, or at least I think I do. Some teachers were kind to me, offered tidbits I wrote down in my notebook, and some of those sparkly trinkets led me down paths toward my voice, my voracious need to research and riff, away from things like clichés, and ho-hum, con- viction-less "this is how it really happened" earnestness, and cheesy gimmicks. They said things like *imitate Whitman, not your freaking classmates!*

Most of what they said I swear by. But will their (now my) tricks work for you? When you don my hat top, will rabbits stream from the back of your coat? Who the hell knows?! But I can say this: when it comes to being a poet, think cicada. Seventeen-year cicada. Figure seventeen years is about what it takes to lie dormant in the ground (not exactly dormant: see below) beneath the tree you will ascend, shirk off your final molt, and belt out the best kind of poesy. As a nymph you will pass through four stages (instars 1-4) before proudly and deserv- edly being crowned Poet Laureate of your Condo/Thatched Roof Hut/ Sidewalk/Back Stoop/Local Watering Hole/Dumpster Alley:

Instar 1: Write about 7,000 really bad poems.

Instar 2: Write another 7,000, real stinkers.

Instar 3: While you are doing all this writing, read every poem you can get your hands on, new and old, last week to beginning of written language. Your mission is to find poems you fall in love with, wish you wrote, poems that give you extreme envy, poems that fool you into thinking you could write one at least as good.

Instar 4: This is the final phase before adulthood. Start sending out your work. Live for the rejections that offer glimmers of encouragement, but expect those to be as common as a cicada trill in December. Read more poems. Write a poem an editor scrawls *almost* across. Stick that poem and his one barely-legible word on your fridge. Talk to that editor each morning as you pour milk into your Life.

Instar 5: Your first acceptance. Now, climb to a nice sunny spot, cling to the bark, and sing it, baby, sing it! If you're not exalted, if you don't feel the wait was worth it, you just weren't meant to be a cicada.

Does seventeen years seem like a long time? Are you feeling impatient? Okay, then—go be a dragonfly. Dragonflies are born in water; they spend about four years swimming around, getting fat on mosquitoes, flies, bees, wasps, and even sometimes butterflies. Be the aquatic dragon: feast on Yeats' bees, Keats's wasps, and Patiann Rogers' butterflies. Make a Strand, Rich, Hayden, Stafford, Clifton sandwich. Slather it with Hillman's mayonnaise, Hacker's mustard. Once you're good and fat on Hass roast beast and Siken hash, on Lockwood linguine, it's time to molt and emerge, a little sooner than seventeen years, but still enough time to croak a decent tune thanks to your crash-course eclectic browsing. Now you can add to the canon poems that are part of the great chain of literary conversation that begins with *Gilgamesh* and continues headlong into Tupac, Cathy Park Hong, Marcus Wicker, poems that zing us awake with startlingly newness that also sounds vaguely familiar, their music and their muscle, their verve-y verbs, their bracing maneuvers, their jolting juxtapositions all making us feel more alive.

But here's the thing about the cicada and dragonfly metaphors: once you're out of the dirt or the pond, you can't go back. What you need is a two-way avenue—to dip back into your own baptismal waters, sniff the primal duff, return to replenish your stock, to nymphasize anew. What you really need to be is a steelhead. Yes, a *steelie*. A sea-run rainbow. You wanted to be a rainbow child, and now you get to be one—but also a rainbow adult, because you're a special kind of fish, you're *anadromous*, which means you go both ways—out to sea, back to your home, that rich source where you must keep returning to for more.

While you're digging, dining, and swimming through the next thousand years of poem-making, keep the tradition verdant and supple by keeping in mind: (1) rules are meant to be learned, then shirked; (2) always err on the side of overshooting your wad; (3) don't let anyone tell you it can't be done, including, most of all, changing the way people think, live, care, and act. In this way you will keep poetry vibrant, shaking to-and-fro like the raucous, untamable creature it is.

Works Cited

Heaney, Seamus. *Beowulf: A New Verse Translation* (Bilingual Edition). W .W. Norton, 2001.

Martha Silano

Ode to Frida Kahlo's Eyebrows

Cult of the brow ascending like a condor,
of refusal to bow to the whimsy of busy tweezers.
From follicle to follicle, freedom unfurls.
Brow most buxom. Ferret brow.
Brow channeling Hieronymus Boschian shenanigans.
Brow championing Duchampian high jinx.
Brow side-skirting ye olde pot o wax.
Brow hobnobbing with Salvadori Dali's mustache.
Mink stole brow; brow I-stole-it-from-a-rodent.
Brow suggesting a profuse, gargantuan beard.
Circus-circuit brow.
Brow that never shook hands with laser.
Most inexplicable brow, most unpixelated.
Bad luck black kitten brow on the prowl.
Mercury in retrograde brow.
Brow undaunted by a John Deere tractor.
Brow the embodiment of national glory.
Brow the mystic mestiza, but brow also
weeping with dislodged fetus, with loss and forlornness.
Brow a come-hither furry viper.
Brow the little known Black Shag Slug.
Brow the unretractable bewhiskered tongue.
Brow the fleecy fluke, tufted cobra, downy leech.
Brow the dark secret of the fastidiously plucked,
that perpetual raised-brow surprise.
Brow surprising, but unsurprised.
Brow the prismatic lion in the wardrobe when you were expecting
beige scarves.
Brow adding a bristly flourish to bright Tehuana dress.
Sing holy praises to the insistence of the brow.

Sit down and write a letter to the core beliefs of the brow.
Knit a sweater to the milagro-like votivity of the brow.
Conjure new words to praise the liftingness of brow.
Flamenco to the mural-worthiness of the brow.
Praise god for the untamability of the brow.
Brow most steadfast. Brow on endless loop,
brow most perennial, most acanthus.
Brow aching yet soaring like an unruffled raven.
Unamputated brow.
Brow never renouncing its femininity.
Feminine brow donning its midnight suit.
Brow the corpse that proves the path to the next.
Brow never resting in peace.
Long live the flourish of the stalwart, seaward sooty gull in every
self-portrait.
Long live the childlike exuberance of the feisty, the feral. Long live
the monkeys
and parrots, perched beside the unwieldy, the emblematic.
Long live those wooly-bear wonders worthy of worship,
like two black wings—signature smudges left by the pig
twirling on a spit *todos los dias, todas las noches*.

Summons and Petition for Name Change

Abelmosk. Abracadabra. Abruzzi. Absolute.
Bonzery. Bogan. Love's barometer. Bristly ballerina.
Choo-choo cherry sanctum. Cutie-cute caldera.
Dim sum-my dilberry. Down there Daiquiri.
Ear of Eden. Eminently Earthy. Empress Gensho.
Fandango-ing funnel. Fox foot. Flamingo.
Geranium in the Gate of the Gourd. Gentian's grin.
Hallelujah in the huckleberry. Ho-Ho-Kus.
Inner Inagaddadavida. Ink on the isthmus.
Jupiter's Big Red Spot. Un-January. Jambalaya.
Knit Kit. Kittewake. Kinnick-kinnick. Nether katzenjammer.
Laniferous lability. Hello Kitty lunch box. Lettuce cup asunder.
Mythic mouth. Mama's milk pan melts Emanuel. Maenadic moon.
Name It Not, Why Not? Nemorous nook. Nefertiti's niche.
O'Keefe. Unfrozen o-ring. Open the sunroom window.
Persimmon portal. Passworded pomegranate. Paisy-waisy.
Quaint Quiver. Quaking qat. Unquashable squab.
Rorschach-y rivulets. Ragmatical raven. Electric rabbit.
Susquehanna. Multi-syllabic sizzler. So strawberry.
Too much fun. Tell me another. Tisket. Tasket. Trisket.
Umbilical's prologue. My own undeniable. Under my undies.
Velvet-it's-not. Venus vector. Victory garden. Vroom-vroom.
Webbed Wednesday. Whipped up elixir. Wowie. Wha-wha.
Xizang. Xebec. Anti-xeric. Excitable raptor. Fringy xenon.
Zounds-mound. Spangled zarf. Naughty zloty. Zerk gone berserk.

Sean Singer
Manifesto

1. Create poems that appear simultaneously spontaneous, yet inevitable.
2. Think thoughts whole.
3. Write from impulse and not rules.
4. Care more about what a line is than what a poem is.
5. Cultivate rhythmical energy which equals psychic energy.
6. Make the line itself syntactically interesting.
7. Make the language move; create a sense of double-ness; celebration & confrontation; rhythm of expecting.
8. Write with lyricism but also truthfulness?—lyricism alone is not what makes literature valuable.
9. Use empathic questioning rather than the Socratic method, which is about being a bully.
10. Cultivate psychological sturdiness; do not specialize in pain.
11. Write without fear of ghosts (parents, authority figures).
12. Write poems that people need, not that they praise.
13. Be courageous enough to put anything clear and un-evasive down on paper.
14. The page is a surface not a space. The words articulate the surface in the way a musician articulates sound. This articulation is the poem not "space." Space is an expression.
15. Be a reader with an active position. Do not be a passive reader. Demand that reading become a creative act.

16. Seek potential for poems to control, destroy, and create
    social institutions.
17. Maintain a general affection for the universe.
18. Poetry is tantamount to thinking.
19. Writing is *process*, not the product.
20. Writing is related to character. If values are sound, the
    writing will be sound.

Ancestors Who Came to New York Harbor From An Extinguished Past

Ellis Island is a little ochre stone
at the bottom of a cloud.

I'm not furrier staring at the fox-colored
sunset. I'm not a women's shoe salesman

going from happiness to unhappiness
and then from unhappiness back to happiness.

Clothed in black wool like black castles
sparks flew off their lapels in a blossoming town.

Think of Jews envying chocolates and cheeses,
their eyes speaking piles of lady's-shoe-heelism

then become worms in an absent city floating
in the inky tea and a silver evening.

On Kazimierz street there's a bar called Singer.
Its sofa pillows, leafy wallpaper, and velvets

remind us that we constantly peer
into fathoms of unfathomednesses.

A slender girl in mulberry stockings
has proven that the dead have a homeland

among the arcades. She's a clairvoyant
of human vapor, the grey spine of a penciled world.

Sean Singer

Embers of Smoldering Homes

It is a major war from
a manufacturing plant
near Ciudad Juárez, a concrete
dust smell from the maquiladoras
cools. There is a pool
of liquid forming
on the stone floor.
When Érika Gándara, the only
cop in Guadalupe Distrito Bravos
was killed the buzzards
were fucking in the wind.
See the brown ribs poking
through the side
of the hound, behind
the broken refrigerator.
The dog is looking for a guaco
leaf, or Saint Teresa.
She has not been seen
since two days before
Christmas. A painting
of the black Mary is wrapped
in plastic wrap, next to the rifle.
Who else is wrapped
in plastic, like drug baggies
or a piece of flesh: Praxédis, Leticia,
Esperanza, Hermila, Felicitas,
Lourdes, Elvira, Gabriela, Elsa Luz . . .
The body has been in the desert
for at least nine days.
A wire chicken coop,

a plaster wall, she vests herself
and waits for you like a hand
stripped of a moving world.
A hand stripped of a moving
world waits for you.
It snaps its fingers
on 2 and 4, a "black snap"
or a sponginess encased
in desire. The fleshy leaves
of the agave bend a white
feather on a girl's brow.
The goatskin deflates
by the opening where,
lashed to itself, she pulls
back her flat breath,
her brittle and meager
clavicle unscrew the pain.
A niña's rose black edge
stumps the coroner
who says something is striking
me, my chrome raindrop,
my jacaranda, pouch of bone.
In Dublin, Ohio,
a sortie of jackals
split the scissors behind the mask
mouth and "cut loose"
for a long needle-devouring night
into the rawhide axis
of dawn, of dung and ashes.
If the word Mexico means
"Place at the Center of the Moon"
then these fabric fireflies
and jutting hips are perfumed
honeyed vibrato moans
and the manic cartels

slice their own heads,
cancer-eaten, like a faceless jaw
snapping the desert moon.
We didn't meet in Mexico's
dark carbon, stretching palpitations
in black armor but a wooden
column of the archangel
who witnesses casually
the teporochos who eat genitals
and fuck watermelons.
When you take the last bus
to Piedras Negras a bullet
has struck the remaining tissue
not of livestock or bodyguard
but the moon's own leather aorta.

Marcela Sulak
Steel Songs
A Poetry Manifesto

For thousands of years steel, like poems, held a people together, said
who would be left out.
On the Texas rice farm and ranch where I grew up we used **steel
barbed wire** (bobwire) to keep things in that wanted to go out.
During hunting season it kept things (people) out that wanted in.

Steel as barbed wire: recognizes that individual property is based
on a constructed (narrated by barbed wire) distinction between
public and private. That my concept of myself as an *I* defined by my
my is political.

[see Frederick Jackson Turner "Frontier Thesis," see the "Big Die Up
Incident," winter, 1885] [see American Bison, Trail of Tears, Indian
Territory]

Wire cutting became a felony in the United States in 1884, a full
year before a federal law passed to forbid stretching fences across
public domain in 1885.

Were barbed wire not reinforced by narrative, no black men would
have been lynched along the highways of the American chronotope
of the road [see Eula Biss "Time and Distance Overcome," see
"Strange Fruit"]

[see Joy Harjo *Crazy Brave*, see James Baldwin *The Fire Next Time*, see Langston Hughes "The Negro Artist and the Racial Mountain," see Ralph Ellison *The Invisible Man*, see Taha Muhammad Ali *My Happiness Bears No Relation to Happiness*, see Patricia Lockwood, see male reviewers' reviews of *Motherland Fatherland Homeland Sexuals*, see Japanese Internment camps]

Lyrical poetry can be complicit. It is prefaced in the assumption that eye=I.
And that this I is a placeholder the reader slips into.

Steel barbed wire is constructed with two strands of steel wire wrapped around sharp barbs.

It's metaphoric, the way it performs the *two sides of every issue* **theatrical drama of the 21st century.**

The loser gets the barb.

What would steel need to be, need to do to refuse the *two sides to every issue* treatment?

Barbed—along the tops of the prison walls—America, 5% of the world's population and 25% of the world's prison population [see sugar cane, see rum, see slave trade].

Joy Harjo came to speak to me and a few hundred other people in Tel Aviv, and to receive a literary prize. She came despite death threats. She asked, *why were they threatening an American Indian poet with death?*

It is difficult to get the news from poems

but impossible to get the news from headlines.

She said, *I had prepared a speech, but now that I'm here, all I'll say is that I am an American Indian living in Oklahoma, on occupied territory, I believe that poetry and art and the spirit world cannot be bound by borders.*

[see Lee Young Li's theory of eating in "The Cleaving." **Poem as steel fork and knife and poem as fingers**]

I am suggesting that communication on the earth is becoming unbearably polarized. That there are increasingly only two sides to every issue.

(*Are you a victim or a terrorist?* is how my Arab student put it in one of her poems)

I am suggesting that the quality of dialogue has been diminished. That we are reduced to the "dominant narrative" and the other one. I am suggesting that poetry is one of the only means of communication able to resist this simplification of communication.

Because poems are complicated, and steel is malleable.

Narrative bravado: and with the last snip of the wire cutters, the spell was broken and everyone became individuals, which is to say, white, Christian, and mostly male. All the cut barbed wire rolled itself into tumble weeds and blew across the land and gradually disintegrated into its organic elements, and poetry gave way to eco-hiking.

> Here's a joke: A Jew, an Arab, a Creek Indian, a black man, and a gaucho walk into a barb...

Steel as metal file means that you personally might escape, but the prison will remain.

[See Michelle Alexander *The New Jim Crow*, see Ferguson and Michael Brown, see Trayvon Martin and Skittles, see how after *Brown v. Board*

of Education, Philadelphia closes 23 schools in minority
neighborhoods and builds a 400 million dollar prison in 2013].

Steel asks what you gonna do with all that wire? You think we can
afford to just leave it lying around? [handcuffs and knife points and
bullets and aircraft carriers]

[see Lola Ridge, "The Song of Iron," "The Legion of Iron," "Iron
Wine."]

Let's melt it down. Let's melt down the snarls of cut barbed wire all
along the highways of America, from the dangling curls of prison
wire, from the barbed metallic locks Rapunzelled down the private
walls.

Steel wire as voice, an embodied I:

Dort erst tratest du ganz in den Namen, der dein ist,
schrittest du sicheren Fußes zu dir,
schwangen die Hämmer frei im Glockenstuhl deines Schweigens,
[see Paul Celan]

Steel wire as cable in the hands of John A. Roebling, 5,434 parallel
wires of it, arranged in 19 strands. Gathered into 4 main cables to
build a Brooklyn Bridge.

**(Because it is not given to every individual to be an *I* before
they've been a *they*.)**

Poem as strands of wire as voices, each voice a liberation! From a
confined space, gathered. Climb voices climb, but beware the barb!

[See Josef Stella "Brooklyn Bridge 1919," see Walker Evans
"Brooklyn Bridge," Hart Crane's *The Bridge* = the ***virtual completion of
Columbus' efforts to circumvent the world.]***

(Columbus, of course, is another barb)

Instead of two competing narratives that between them clutch the precious barb of pain—5,432 strands, the difference between a bridge and barbed wire.

Avera

crossing, violation

In Venezuela, we could whack the heads off these empty wine bottles, plant
their bottoms in fresh cement so their jagged teeth would flash
between the rich
and those of the poor unemployed by the rich. If we were still
in Germany, there'd be a pragmatic plastic bin labeled *colored glass*,
and there
they'd sleep it off, till someone hauled them to the rubber belt
they'd ride for free, be scrubbed and dried. They'd open
their mouths and be filled again. If we were still in Austin
or South Philly we'd be laughing so hard when they fell, we'd
gather their shards, and with mirrors (because the more
the merrier) and plastic glo-in-the-dark saints
we'd make the guys who piss against the walls at night
something nice to look at;

as Henry Ford said, art should be something for every day. Most
workers on
large public projects in Mesopotamia got one liter of beer
a day. On the occasion of Queen Pu-abi's death (daily
allotment, six liters, with silver, gold and lapis straws, cased with
marsh reeds) twelve chamber maids, five male armed guards and two
groomsmen were thrown
a banquet to die for. Literally. Had
I been there I would have looked longest at the rams rendered
in gold, silver and lapis lazuli—each raised on hind
legs, nibbling a shrub—coffee? At some point that
night, I would have dipped my cup into a copper
pot, like everyone else, and drunk it. The effect
was irreversible.

It's true my mother's angry children made me keep their vineyards
    while my own
I had not kept. But lately I've found myself possessed of stone jars
    full of
sweet and of breath that hovers just above the earth awhile. When
I taste it I don't know what is earth and what air, what is water, what
    fire, who
my mother's angry children are, where *never* ends where I
begin and what Pu-abi did with the key
to the death pit where the banquet was. The only thing worse
than being unloved is being loved above all others.
Ayin-bet-reysh pronounced *Avera*——means violation,
means moving, since at a certain point it's hard to
stop. Moving, from one word to the next because ayin-bet-reysh,
pronounced *Ivrit*, is language

or "Hebrew" and a state of existence if you happen to be Avram,
the first Hebrew, crossing a river from his and Queen Pu-abi's
hometown Ur into Canaan. Since then every age of wonder
has its own body of water, and the inconsolable who discover what
they crossed was sometimes only the usual kind of water,
which is why Baudelaire said *always be drunk*;
be drunk means be emptied or else filled, almost all the way,
but never at the same time. A tooth in the mouth of the
Gulf of Mexico, my grandfather reminds me
of Noah. First thing upon disembarking, his
native village obliterated, he planted
himself a vineyard, too.

Marcela Sulak

Union

Two small onions filled the eye-sockets of Ramses IV who lay stiff, as
    if awake
in the rusty crook of the Nile's arm (which, when viewed
from an aerial photo, resembles a scar
in the Valley of the Kings). Night falls swiftly there
and artists were assigned inspirations that endured longer than
    their lives,
precision carving tools, and strips
of cloth combed from the local weeds.

Onions in chest cavities, attached to the soles of the feet, in the
    pelvis, along
bald legs, molded in the ears, poised the expectant
body for its next breath in a bold pre-furnished
afterworld. They were red skinned, the same color as
Ramses IV's legendary hair. Their name
came when the onion-shaped letter o

slipped into *union*. A union is something invisible. Under
    investigation
it falls apart. But it's somewhat comforting to
me that even loss is never completely effaced.
After Pompeii burned, the onion bulbs remained
as cavities beneath the scorched ground. Now draw me into your
    mouth and blow
me out, because I don't want to
be immortal, but thoroughly spent.

Maureen Thorson
"A Poetics of Responsibility"

A poem should be responsible—to itself and to its audience. That doesn't mean it must be political, that it must aim squarely at the righting of social wrongs. While poems often, I think, have more power in that regard than we might think, a love poem is as valid as a protest poem. (Sometimes it *is* a protest poem). Wallace Stevens—no activist—nonetheless thought that the poet's role is "to help people to live their lives." In pursuit of that broad mandate, we need not ask that all poems be in the business of righting injustices. But it's not too much to ask that poems not commit them.

No poem is a private utterance. When Walt Whitman shouted his barbaric yawp over the roofs of the world, it was not an anonymous cry into the darkness. It was his yawp; it was addressed to the world. This relationship of poet and audience governs a poem's understanding and reception; they form the context in which the poet, in Joan Retallack's words, may "behave with concern and courage as an artist." Often we focus on the courage; the concern should be remembered as well.

We've all heard stories of writers who regularly mine their lives for their work and who, because of how they go about it, aren't on speaking terms with half of their loved ones. Speaking does not, of course, deny other people their own speech. It is not as though there is only so much language to go around and every poem written removes some bit of the available material. But for a poet not to think about how a poem affects its subjects and its audience—whether the message is worth the price of the method—is to fail, utterly, to "behave with concern and courage." A few years ago, I began writing poems about the sometimes-difficult, sometimes-ecstatic days in which my husband and I began to build our life together. When I started to read those poems to audiences, a funny thing happened. Based on what I had read, people thought that they knew *him*, without his ever having said a word. And the poems were not always "fair"—they reflected my own view and my own biases, emotions that have altered with time. And so, as I edited the poems toward publication, I vetted them with my husband to make sure that in telling my own story, I wasn't misrepresenting his.

Poets sometimes like to think themselves apart and above, but responsibility attaches to anyone who puts words out in the world. You may wish to claim that because of the method of production—that the poem is "found language," for example—that you are "out of the process" and cannot be held accountable. But merely asserting that you are being reportorial—that what you are doing isn't, in fact, art, but a sort of mechanistic rebroadcasting of material already present in the world—is no defense. After all, it's you who's chosen what to report.

While the writer who uses his family and friends as material may cause ripples among his intimates, his larger audience may remain untroubled. The poetic movements of the twentieth century left readers half-expecting every poem to be personal, to air the poet's dirty laundry. And a stranger's pain is delectably abstract. But what of objectively violent material? Racist language? Sexist or homophobic speech? There are good and useful ends for such material—to witness, to make aware, to call others to action, to explore solutions. But such material may reproduce trauma, rather than comment on or heal it. It may wound without discrimination.

You should be satisfied with your own motives and methods. Said plainly, it might sound hokey, but it's true nonetheless: Words have meaning; they have power. And this means you can never detach yourself from responsibility for the words you wield. Be loud, be critical. Be sarcastic and mean and wild. But be prepared to be criticized for being those things, be prepared to defend yourself for being those things. Accept and embrace that as part of your responsibility. And if you can't, it's time to consider why you're writing things that you aren't willing to stand behind.

Works Cited

Stevens, Wallace. *The Necessary Angel: Essays on Reality and the Imagination*. Knopf, 1951, p. 29.

Whitman, Walt. "Song of Myself," *Poetry Foundation*, https://www.poetryfoundation.org/poems-and-poets/poems/detail/45477. Accessed 30 October 2016.

Retallack, Joan. *The Poethical Wager*. University of California Press, 2003, pp. 3–4.

Maureen Thorson

Exploding Violet

Kali is your girl,
you know, tongues
and hands afire:
That sleek little belt

of lolling skulls.
What she desires
is a look inside you—
a documentary impulse

that charms, alarms,
but girlfriend's got ADD,
she's all smiles
one second,

rotting jowls the next.
You've come to expect
the purple-hooded blouse,
the lurid attempt

to command
both respect and subjects,
but the thick and hairy foliage
is something new—

her bit of fun.
Reversing fortunes
is what you do
when you're holy,

a sacred automaton
that swallows
all devotion
like a whale,

like an orchid,
waxy-lipped
and summoning
strength from what is dead.

Et in arcadia ego,
she laughs,
rocking out
in the dripping canopy,

roots bound
into the branches.
There are crucial benefits
to mortality,

and she's got the goods,
sensuous floral
fragrance overlaid
with vegetal decay,

petals shot
with veins of rage,
chromatic and choleric,
the cycling spectrum

of desire. *You can't
rise up unless you fall*,
she says, hooking
a sugar skull

past her velvet throat.
Immortality is a dull
immensity. Rotting's better.
Let's hit the mall.

Rocking the Pathetic Fallacy

SER PERMANENTE

A half-grasped sign
forgoes commercial purpose,
becomes an omen—

                    end times ahead.

Sure, the glass is full right now...
              but I've seen it drain before.

          Anyway, I don't want to explain
what I meant by *this*,
why I don't feel like doing *that*.

The French will tell you:

          "One train may conceal another."

Having passed April's low hurdles, I feel you like a corner.

The shrill piano means
              something's getting closer.

Outside the window,
              rain gathers up its thunder, batters
the mint from its pot.

Maureen Thorson

I glance down the corridor—
      I see—

      the look in your eyes that is *yes*.

The hope that I hope I obtain.

Afaa Weaver
What Lies Inside Us
Connectedness in Language and Being

The twentieth century was a time when English and European languages reached the height of their influence over the colonized world, and then began to fall back as languages and cultures began to claim their sovereign space in consciousness. At the same time, psychology and medicine revealed the subconscious, while physics revealed the subatomic world. The twentieth century was a bursting open, like a cornucopia of fresh fruit and flowers bursting, blossoming, and then breaking into the twenty-first century's fractal realities of the digital world, where anything can be real, and the real is a matter of personal choice. We can reach each other in microseconds, but there is also the sense of growing more and more distant from one another. Intimacy is a secret best kept in the mouth of God, the space where poets have always lived, and it is in this century that we begin to sound that space with deed and title we will never lose.

Translation and travel have made it possible for us to assemble a new vibrancy in language and experience. It is here that we begin. It is here that we let loose the poetic consciousness to assemble a new set of selves, not in the sense of colonizing the spirit but of opening it, of making of the mind what it is, the breathing membrane of sentience. Early twentieth-century avant-garde was an attempt to outdo science in revealing the mind. As science enters neuroscience, it is the poets who have the most profound access to the mind.

This is the age of not one language or a few but of many struggling to live, and in that struggle the poetry of the most intense human needs will speak. We will establish a new cognitive through poetic consciousness. We will assume the prior knowledge of the spirit. We will connect the nexus of all languages that is latent inside every human being, and use it in our individual lives as the first artists of language as we connect that subconscious nexus to the outer world of language and culture.

It is a poetry I can glimpse faintly now and one I know will arise as science meets metaphysics in our time, as poetry holds the world to the imperatives of the deep compassion human beings can have for one another. In this way we will be affirmed, if we realize who we are and defend our function in human consciousness.

City of Eternal Spring

My mind rises up as the silos of interchanges,
streams, passages of myself in floating layers
so nothing can connect, and I dream emptiness
on ships sailing to new places for new names,
this ship my hands cupped in front of me,
a beggar's bowl, a scooped out moon, a mouth
opened to make noiseless screams, to arrange,
to begin, to break through to stop my arrogance,
believing what I touch, see, feel, hear, taste make
a case for being alive, so I can stop believing what
happens when a caterpillar dreams itself beautiful.

What cannot be is suddenly what I was made
to believe can never be, fibers growing in illegal
spaces between layers of who I am and I wake
from nightmares that come at night or in the day,
memories of being betrayed gathering like iron
threads to make a prison where fibers of a miracle
of light crack open in a seed inside love to let me
dream a body inside this body with structures
that breathe and know one another so I rise
from thought to be being beyond thought
with energy as breath, a world with eyes
opening inside the light, inside knowing,
inside oneness that appears when the prison
frees me to know I am not it and it is not me.

Afaa Weaver

To Those Who Would Awaken

It will happen like this for many of you,
the house suddenly too much, the garden so full
you go out, maybe thinking of the way the earth gives
under your feet, the water makes circles around them
if you have to cross a river, leaves and branches lift
up and then brush against you when you have
crossed, these things or the very structure of things,
the making of the hip joint, electrical plots in the
heart, thalamus sending reminders to the moving,
you looking up into the still wings of gliding crows
on this day when you know in one second there
is the power to give things new names, so you decide
this is not leaving but returning, that ends are
middles or that there are no points, no time,
so by the time you are miles away from leaving
it is only the eternal very first moment of anything,
making a pound cake from scratch, moving your
hand across the hem of a new skirt, the slight fear
and tremble when a sudden sound hits your wall, like
children throwing the ball against the fire escape
until it rattles like an empty skeleton, the hot shower
where you are alone until the memories step
in with you, deep solitude of living alone, falling
to where you are connected with everything, and
it happens, the stepping out, mind full of seeing
yourself move out into the world without difference
so you can see every move you make is a change
in the current, the arrangement of patterns under a brush,
a twisted calligrapher's stroke, all these things, walking
while the bones of who you are become roots.

Jillian Weise
Biohack Manifesto

It is terrible to be trapped at DEF CON
with not even Ray Kurzweil's
daughter to gaze upon
I know some of you wish
I would go wherever
my people go, the factory,
physical therapy, a telethon

No! says my mentor
Not this. This is too angry

This is too much about
Not that. Not that

I like to hack, sometimes,
the Hebrew Bible

I don't think my mentor hacks
the Bible b/c it has too much
lame deaf blind circumcised in it

Not that. Not that in poetry
Didn't we already have

Judd Woe? He was so good to us
so good and sad and sorry

The great thing about Judd Woe
is that now we don't have to
keep looking for a disabled poet
We got him

Everybody together now: We got him
Thank Y H W H he's a man

I am so relieved, aren't you?
I am so cock-blocked, aren't you?

Here I am at the cobbler

Please, please can you make
all my high heels into wedges

Here I am at Wal-Mart

Please, please can you make
your children stop following me

Here I am at Advanced Prosthetics

Please, please can you
change my settings

THIS IS NOT POETRY, they said

Be happy with what we give you
We got you

Insurance: You are allowed ten socks/year

Insurance: You are not allowed to walk in oceans

Insurance: If you had fought for us, if you
had lost your leg for us, for freedom, then
we would cover the leg that walks in oceans

AND WHY IS IT ALWAYS A POEM IS A WALK?

A poem is like a walk
A poem is like going on a walk
A walk is like a poem
I was walking the other day and a poem tripped me

Don't leave
Don't I have any other ideas
Be a man, mortality, zip it

Call in the aubades
I wish I would read an aubade
Is it morning yet? This manifesto
is so so long. Too angry
Who you bangin' on my door?

JUDY GRAHN

Thank Y H W H . It was getting hot in here
Ray Kurzweil's daughter is in Hawaii
I was about to give up

Yes
Yes
I know

I am trying to walk the treadmill
My leg beeps at 3 mph

This is the conference for hackers
Can somebody hack me
Can somebody change my settings

Yes
Yes
I know

JENNY HOLZER

So glad you could make it
Come in, JUDY is here
What do ya'll do with all the men in our heads

Yes
Yes
It is terrible

My people are just trying to get born
like please don't test us
we are going to fail
and the test comes back
and says YOUR BABY IS FUCKED

JUDY, JENNY, I have been your student faithfully

I have kissed some ass, tho, hoping
if they like me enough—what
if they like me enough—why

JUDY, do you need a coaster?
Thy cup runneth over

The glass slipper, amenities
The manifesto must go on

BIOHACK IT

CUT ALL OF IT, my mentor says
This is not poetry

My mentor says: A poem is a walk
Get well soon, I pray for you
Must go   Poem about co-ed
virility   aging   dahlias

Recurrent word to describe beauty
hacked from the Hebrew Bible: Ruddy

Don't leave   In the morning
I will vacuum this up   Scansion, feet

I am sorry if you offended me
Role of disabled artist:
Always be sorry

Semi Semi Dash

The last time I saw Big Logos he was walking
to the Quantum Physics Store to buy magnets.
He told me his intentions. He was wearing

a jumpsuit with frayed cuffs. I thought the cuffs
got that way from him rubbing them against
his lips but he said they got that way

with age. We had two more blocks to walk.
"Once I do this, what are you going to do?"
he asked. "I wish you wouldn't do it," I said.

Big Logos bought the magnets and a crane
delivered them to his house. After he built
the 900-megahertz superconductor, I couldn't go

to his house anymore because I have all kinds
of metal in my body. I think if you love someone,
you shouldn't do that, build something like that,

on purpose, right in front of them.

To Forget Mark Dicklip

Because I for one was done
with Mark Dicklip, I went
to the brane-world where
I had some adjustments, made
some friends. There were aisles
with fluorescent congress.
I took the optogenetic option.
The Fearless Leader said:
"Tartle," which means *come up
on me*. He in his kerchief
and I in my glow. "A light
shines from you," he said,
and a light really did, out top
of my head. "I want to hit it."
But did he like the light
or the bitch inside? Always
the same dope. He called me
Lil Blue. There were no phones.
He called me in my head
from his head. It got loud.
Because I for one was done
with Mark Dicklip, I attended.
All members met. "Is anyone
concerned that we don't
know the shape we're in?"
said Math. "Good shape."
"Fearless shape." "Constant
control of bowels shape."
Other shapes were discussed.
"No," said Math. "The universe.

Is it a doughnut?" Your group,
said I to the Leader, is whack.
Why care I what shape I'm in
long as I cease to take shape
when you bandit me. Except
don't smile. You scare a bitch.
What do you think this is?

Look back it's all so fluently
reckless. Look front it's all
so overdone. I woke mornings
to headache and fog. I didn't
eat right. Didn't sleep right.
I walked the aisles. Was everly
walking. "Maybe you should
have fought a little harder,"
said my motherboard. "Maybe
if you loved Mark Dicklip
you would have fought harder."
Math, he was a querulous fucker
with big doppers and a hair.
"Lil Blue," said he. "How do
optogenetics treat you? I read
in *Post-American* that it cost
a pretty crux. Does it work?"
"Lil Blue," said Math, right up
on my cart. I'm still here, said I.
"Do you think it's an equation
I could get into with you? An X?
Or any old unknown?"
I took his quest seriously.
There was talk of probability.
The position has been filled, said I.
By the Leader. He is often
in my head quoting Tony Robbins—

Don't say, "I'm feeling good."
Say, "I'm feeling energized."
I'm feeling glocked. Scatty.
"You're not doing it right," said he.
Since it's not wise to play
autoerotics into next year's
parties, I employ The Leader.
Engager of skull's compost.
Bone for cross-bone. He in
his kerchief and I in my glow.
Goodnight I'm going to bed beside
the Leader and no Mark Dicklip.
Goodnight Prof. Moore and Weezy.
I also want to say: Goodnight
Ed Dorn—pleased to meet
your *Twenty-four Love Scorned
Sonnets*—and goodnight
motherboard. Leader. Tartle.
Tartle. Can you hear me?
"We can all hear you."
When finally did I sleep
Math woke me and we said:
You wouldn't know if you were
in it. I am in it. You might be
in it. I am in it. That's what you
think. I know it. Somebody
told you you're in it. Still,
he wanted to know, what shape?

Valerie Wetlaufer
Inscribing the Domestic Daily

I believe in a poetry that is expansive. There is room for all differ-
ent aesthetics in the poetry world, so I don't intend this to be a mani-
festo of what poetry is *not*; rather I seek to describe the kinds of poetry
that most interest *me*, rather than to dictate some aesthetic principle
to be applied to all.

I seek after a poetry of the every day. A way to strive toward art even
in the seemingly mundane. I am trying to find a way to fit my life into
poetry. So much of the daily work of life—housekeeping and childrear-
ing, the work still mostly relegated to women's unpaid labor—often
isn't seen as appropriate for poems. So many days I spend sick in bed
from one chronic disease or another. Those days are a wash of pain.
Staring up at the ceiling fan. Slowly turning over, seeking a more
bearable position, brain foggy from medication. When I'm lucky, I'm
able to scratch out a few lines.

In 2010, I started writing a poem a day, and these daily details first
gained entrance into my poems, where previously I avoided anything
domestic, assuming poetry had to be something grand and external. I
still write a draft of something every day (my rule is that it has to be at
least 10 lines), and I now welcome the quotidian into my work. I think
about a grand tradition of women writing about their lives, and the
details that preoccupy them, such as Virginia Woolf, and Gertrude Stein,
both of whom include the magnitude of every day details in their work,
from Mrs. Dalloway's flowers to Stein's catalogue of domesticity in *Tender*

Buttons. In *Midwinter Day*, one of my favorite books, Bernadette Mayer records her process of writing while living. This book length poem was written in one day as an attempt to record everything that happened. For Mayer, this included work frequently characterized as unintellectual because domestic. She details the minutiae of everyday life while she cooks, takes care of her children, goes to the grocery store, and generally goes about her daily routine. At the same time that she records the playful babble of her daughters, she meditates on her literary precursors. Throughout the text, Mayer is concerned with female literary influence and ancestry, even cataloguing her lineage of female writers. Though she doesn't include Dorothy Wordsworth in her list, another influence on my work, the two writers are engaged in similar projects, and both can be situated in a tradition of female writers composing marginal forms. Wordsworth's *Grasmere and Alfoxden Journals*, never intended for publication, exist as a poetic inscription of her daily life with her brothers. Structurally, the journals both satisfy and frustrate the reader's desire for linear narrative, telling embedded stories but abruptly concluding or interrupting them to record whatever else happened. They are discontinuous, episodic, and fragmentary, responsive to the randomness and arbitrariness of events, not the self of her brother, or a unified rational or intentional depiction of self. The self in Dorothy's journals is one embodied in a routine of physical labor, of the daily production of food and clothing and shelter. A self built, as were many other women's selves of the time, on a model of affiliation rather than a model of individual achievement. She constructs subjectivity through detail, physical embodiment, energetic activity and enacted consciousness. Dorothy *is* what she sees and does and eats and feels and speaks and writers.

Both Mayer and Wordsworth taught me to question the notion that the quotidian is something to be transcended. Instead, it can be celebrated in verse, even when it disappoints. I seek to trouble the idealized idea of home through portraits of homes both haven and horror, by investigating the domestic sublime, creating a mise en abîme rooted not in the gothic nor nature but in dailiness. The body enters the poem in different ways in this domestic daily life, alongside the physical labor of keeping the house clean and everyone fed. There's both a communal aspect to this daily life, as well as moments of grave solitude. This is not a life in the ivory tower, nor a room of one's own, but a life lived with others, and the recording of how isolating it often is when one is alone in community.

The poems presented here deal directly with experiences of daily life in an associative and fragmentary fashion. They are part of a larger series, which will be in my third book, in-progress, *Bloom & Scruple*. They were also written in a Mayersque style in the midst of living. I am interrupted at the desk writing. The dog needs to go outside.

This is nothing like New York

No sidewalk smear,

but the possum got into the attic again,

& the pipes froze. You were under the house

with the hair dryer this morning trying to thaw them.

Such bright light on the snow:

blinding. On the edges of my mind, a memory

but there is work to be done every day

& no time for nostalgia. I milk the goats and

remember tromping through snow in the city

when I was young. What now is beneath my feet here?

Layers upon layers.   Turn the compost

and break the crust of ice on the water trough.

So much white. A blizzard vortex blowing.

Valerie Wetlaufer

There are things to be done every day

skim the skin from the milk

      shell the peas trim the grass

the children need waking

              wear garments with pockets

for all the things you must carry

      dirty down the colors

         brew the tea strong and black

let the dog in   let the dog out

      your ink-stained hands can accomplish lots

time the contractions   nurse the child

      forget your unpaid labor burdens you

time for the library   time for the stories

      shell the peas

burn the roast   rake the leaves

     pour the coffee   sign papers

try for a moment to remember how to pray

Rachel Zucker
Dear Christine

you don't like cold cuts   on the other hand   you make a funny face & say "you keep
saying that!"   when I make jokes   about being   an old lady   by which you mean to say
"you're not an old lady"   at least I think that's what you mean

                      "When I was your age . . ."

no one said   "deli meats" or "tomfoolery"   that there's oldladyspeak   for cold cuts
& nonsense &   I already said   how you feel about cold cuts   truth is
I've never been   anyone's boss   not even yours   except a little   which is different
than being   someone's mother   totally different   sometimes being   your boss
is a little bit like   being someone's mother   I mean to say   the more authority I have   over you
the smarterthanme   you seem to become   which is confusing   have you noticed this?

                      is this another way of saying

"I'm an old lady"?   or is saying   "I'm an old lady"   a way of   getting you to say
"you keep saying that!"   which is your way of saying   "stop saying that!"   which is a way of
my figuring out   if I'm an old lady   because I'm really not sure   but pretty sure   no one
is suddenly going to say   "hey, you're an old lady now"   which might be helpful   I wouldn't know

another way of saying this is   "I don't have a daughter"

which is true   & someday soon someone in a white coat might say   even though I'm not   trying
to have a daughter   "you'll never have a daughter"   which is another way of saying   I'm an old lady
even though I am someone's mother   not the mother of a young woman like you   or any woman or girl
even my nieces look at me   with a look that says   I'm their uncle's wife   only child you   won't have
nieces nor nephews either   unless you marry into them   & I'm here to tell you   it's not the same

"I'm here to tell you"

is like "deli meats"   it's oldladyspeak for   "I think I know a thing or two"   which is oldladyspeak for "listen here dearie"   which is oldladyspeak for   "sure, yup, since you asked   I do think you should let   that boyfriend of yours   move in with you"   I'm in favor of that   & other towardlove&life decisions   in general & particularly   in this case   because I like   thatboyfriendofyours & the way he seems   to like you   which is   a particularly nice quality   in boyfriends   so don't say I never taught you nothin'   which is something   you'd never say   because you're nice   also don't talk in a vernacularslang or otherwiseway   which is not to say   "humorless"   which is oldladyspeak   for unfunny

what I'm trying to say is

one way I know I'm not   your boss is   I have an opinion about   "that boyfriend of yours" which is   oldladyspeak for   Colin   then again   I've never been   anyone's boss   maybe all bosses have opinions like this   maybe in this way   being a boss is like   being someone's mother which is full of   opinions like   I do not want you   to work in a soap factory   which you were actually doing   until recently &   which reminds me   of what happens   to old horses   which is not something I know anything about   firsthand because   I've always lived in NYC   but I do know   gelatin isn't kosher   it comes from horsehooves   at least that's what   the little yids said   back in the day

I was a yeshiva girl   back in the day   when my teachers said   "back in the day they turned

Jews into soap didn't even have   the decency to use horses"   I think I might be   mixing up

glue&soap   also no vegan would agree with   that use of   the word "decency"   my teachers didn't use

the phrase   "back in the day"   when they talked about   the H'caust   which is   a shanda to joke about

even now   you should have seen   my teachers   they were not really teachers   were shattered survivors

who   shouldn't have been   allowed near children but that's   another kvetch altogether

hey how'd it get so Jewish   in here?

I suppose that's   part of what makes me cry   "oldlady oldlady"   cuz when I am one   no doubt

I'll be   that crazyoldJewishlady   there I go again   anyway   you eat cheese but not

delimeats   I saw you   once eat a little bit of brisket   at my Passover seder   I'll never tell anyone

I just did   I wonder   how many years before   "Passover" & "yeshiva" are   oldladyspeak for

"remember the days when there were Jews?"   my son said   "the Jews should just leave Israel"

"eventually there won't be Jews and that's probably OK"   he said that right before   the recent peacefire   he said

I meant ceasefire   which ended   hours after it began   this is one of   the many problems

with being someone's mother   having to care   what a son says & feels   & feelingresponsible   I bet

you wouldn't say that   even if you thought it   not to me because   for one thing   you're not my daughter

"I knew you when you were just a . . ."

is oldladyspeak for   you were my student   when you were what, 20?   & again at 25?   it's not my job
to keep track of your exact age   was my job to help you write poems which   I'm not sure anyone
can help someone else do   especially since you   were already writing poems   I'm supposed to be
reading   *Deepstep Come Shining*   or writing   a manifesto

crap!

        I just burned a whole pot
of beans   while not reading Wright or writing a manifesto too much Ammons got me   into the habit
it seems   of going on & going on& on   now everything smells "horrid"   which is   oldladyspeak for   sometimes
fuckingbad   everything smells like   burntbeans   in this case because that's what happened
I make up   compoundwords   in honor of you   you do that   in your poems   I never told you to   or told you
not to   some things you can't teach or say   I can say anything   doesn't mean it's useful   or anyone's listening
but you seem to   (cars over gravel outside   none of them my husband)   (a couple calling a lost dog)   I do think
you'll like   being addressed   otherwise not care much   for this poem   will be   too polite   to say so

    would you like me to get to the point?

would you like me   to tell you   the secret of life?   would you like me   to tell you   *you*
who are   my student not anymore   a kind of daughter but kinder   a sort of employee not really
the secret of life is   there isn't one   this is smarter than it sounds   at least I think so   the secret is
everyone's already done everything   felt everything   backintheday & today   are the same   days
but nonetheless   *matter*   it all does whether   Colin moves in or doesn't   if you have babies one day
maybe a daughter   it will be   so sappy & sentimental   nothing new about any of it   except everything
in the fucking world about it   or you can be   a notmother that's another way & OK too   both filled with
sadnessjoyloneliness&   moments   if you're lucky   you've got someone   friend daughter maybe student
either way   one day   you'll burn a whole pot of beans   might be I'm dead by then   but I know
what your kitchen   will smell like   exactly like   which is another way of saying   I might not know
everything   or anything   but I know sometimes having a person like you to write to   is enough

real poem (appellation)

"Writing with My Shoes On" is
a title for a poem. "Then I Did
Something Stupid" is better
for a short story. The trash smells
because living things decompose
isn't the name of anything just
a way of describing these environs.
To say I miss you in French
one says *tu me manques* where
tu means "you." Do the French
miss less because their you is
there before them? Syntactical
high jinks: methinks Americans
don't miss the missed-one
so much as feel how absence
crowds the I. Today my others are
far from me. "I"— is
the name of this feeling.

Racher Zucker

real poem (personal statement)

I skim sadness like fat off the surface
of cooling soup. Don't care about
metaphor but wish it would arrive
me. There's a cool current of air
this hot day I want to ride.
I have no lover, not even my love.
I have no other, not even I.

Contributors

Lisa Ampleman is the author of a book of poetry, *Full Cry* (NFSPS Press, 2013), and a chapbook, *I've Been Collecting This to Tell You* (Kent State University Press, 2012). Her poems have appeared in journals such as *Poetry, Image, Kenyon Review Online, 32 Poems, Poetry Daily,* and *Verse Daily,* and her reviews and prose in *Connotation Press, Diagram, Good Letters, Pleiades,* and *Southeast Review Online.* She is a graduate of the PhD program at the University of Cincinnati.

Sandra Beasley is author of *Count the Waves* (W. W. Norton, 2015); *I Was the Jukebox* (W. W. Norton, 2010), winner of the Barnard Women Poets Prize; and *Theories of Falling* (New Issues Poetry & Prose, 2008), winner of the New Issues Poetry Prize. Honors for her work include an NEA Literature Fellowship, the Center for Book Arts Chapbook Prize, and three DCCAH Artist Fellowships. She is also the author of the memoir *Don't Kill the Birthday Girl: Tales from an Allergic Life* (Crown, 2011). She lives in Washington, D.C., and is on the faculty of the University of Tampa MFA program.

Sean Bishop is the author of *The Night We're Not Sleeping In* (Sarabande, 2014), winner of the Kathryn A. Morton Prize in Poetry. His poems have appeared in *Poetry, Ploughshares, Boston Review, Harvard Review, jubilat, Best New Poets, Alaska Quarterly Review,* and elsewhere, and his essays on literary publishing have appeared on the blogs of *Ploughshares* and *Virginia Quarterly Review.* He coordinates the MFA and Fellowship programs at the University of Wisconsin-Madison, where he teaches poetry writing and creative writing pedagogy. He is at work on a book-length erasure of Charles Darwin's *On the Origin of Species.*

Susan Briante is the author of two books of poetry: *Utopia Minus* (Ahsahta Press, 2011) and *Pioneers in the Study of Motion* (Ahsahta Press, 2007). Her next collection of poems, *The Market Wonders,* will be published in 2016, also by Ahsahta Press. She is an associate professor of Creative Writing at the University of Arizona.

Stephen, or Stephanie, Burt is Professor of English at Harvard and the author of several books of poetry and literary criticism, among them *Belmont* (2013), *Close Calls with Nonsense* (2009), and the forthcoming *Advice from the Lights* (2017), all from Graywolf Press.

Jen Campbell is the author of the *Sunday Times* bestselling *Weird Things Customers Say in Bookshops* series (Little Brown, 2012/2013) and *The Bookshop Book* (Little Brown, 2014). She is also an award-winning poet and short story writer. Her poetry pamphlet 'The Hungry Ghost Festival' is published by The Rialto (2012) and she runs a Youtube channel over at www.youtube.com/jenvcampbell where she discusses all things books.

Kara Candito is the author of *Spectator* (University of Utah Press, 2014), winner of the Agha Shahid Ali Poetry Prize, and *Taste of Cherry* (University of Nebraska Press, 2009), winner of the Prairie Schooner Book Prize in Poetry.

Bruce Cohen's poems have appeared in such literary periodicals as *AGNI, The Georgia Review, The Harvard Review, The New Yorker, Ploughshares, Poetry,* and *The Southern Review* as well as being featured on *Poetry Daily* & *Verse Daily*. He has published five volumes of poetry: *Disloyal Yo-Yo* (Dream Horse Press), which was awarded the 2007 Orphic Poetry Prize, *Swerve* (Black Lawrence Press), *Placebo Junkies Conspiring with the Half-Asleep* (Black Lawrence Press) and most recently *No Soap, Radio!* (Black Lawrence Press). His most recent manuscript, *Imminent Disappearances, Impossible Numbers & Panoramic X-Rays*, was awarded the 2015 Green Rose Prize from New Issues Press and was published in 2016. A recipient of an individual artist grant from the Connecticut Commission on Culture & Tourism, he joined the Creative Writing faculty at the University of Connecticut in 2012.

Erica Dawson is the author of two collections of poetry: *The Small Blades Hurt* (Measure Press, 2014) and *Big-Eyed Afraid* (Waywiser Press, 2007). Her poems have appeared in *Best American Poetry, Harvard Review, Virginia Quarterly Review*, and many other journals and anthologies. She is an Associate Professor of English and Writing at The University of Tampa, where she serves as Director of the Low-Residency MFA in Creative Writing.

Sean Thomas Dougherty is the author or editor of 14 books including *Double Kiss: Contemporary Writers on the Art of Billiards* (Mammoth Books, 2016), *All You Ask for Is Longing: Poems 1994-2014* (BOA Editions, 2014) and *Scything Grace* (Etruscan Press, 2013). His awards include two Pennsylvania Arts Council Fellowships in Poetry, a Fulbright Lectureship, and an appearance in *Best American Poetry 2014*. He now works in a pool hall in Erie, PA, and tours widely for performances.

Jehanne Dubrow is the author of five poetry collections, including most recently *The Arranged Marriage* (University of New Mexico Press, 2015), *Red Army Red* (Northwestern University Press, 2012), and *Stateside* (Northwestern University Press, 2010). Her work has appeared in *Virginia Quarterly Review, The New England Review, Ploughshares,* and *The New York Times Magazine.*

Rebecca Morgan Frank is the author of two collections of poems, *The Spokes of Venus* (Carnegie Mellon 2016) and *Little Murders Everywhere* (Salmon 2012), a finalist for the Kate Tufts Discovery Award. Her poems have appeared such places as *Ploughshares, Harvard Review, New England Review,* and *Guernica,* and she is the recipient of the Poetry Society of America's Alice Fay di Castagnola Award. She is co-founder and editor of the online magazine *Memorious* and the Jacob Ziskind Poet-in-Residence at Brandeis University.

Elisa Gabbert is the author of *L'Heure Bleue, or the Judy Poems* (Black Ocean, 2016), *The Self Unstable* (Black Ocean, 2013) and *The French Exit* (Birds LLC, 2010).

Hannah Gamble is the author of *Your Invitation to a Modest Breakfast* (Fence Books, 2012), selected by Bernadette Mayer for the 2011 National Poetry Series. She has performed her work at the Pitchfork music festival, the Chicago Art Institute, The Chicago MCA, and as part of the Clark Street Bridge arts series in association with FCB Global. In 2014, Gamble was awarded a Ruth Lilly and Dorothy Sargent Rosenberg Poetry fellowship from the Poetry Foundation. She lives in Chicago.

Noah Eli Gordon teaches in the MFA Program in Creative Writing at the University of Colorado at Boulder, where he currently directs Subito Press. He is the author of several books, including the recent *The Word Kingdom in the Word Kingdom* (Brooklyn Arts Press, 2015).

David Groff's book *Clay* (Trio House Press, 2013) was chosen by Michael Waters for the Louise Bogan Award. His first book *Theory of Devolution* (University of Illinois Press, 2002) was selected by Mark Doty for the National Poetry Series. He has coedited the Lambda-winning *Who's Yer Daddy?: Gay Writers Celebrate Their Mentors and Forerunners* (University of Wisconsin Press, 2013) and *Persistent Voices: Poetry by Writers Lost to AIDS* (Alyson, 2010). He received his MFA from the Iowa Writers Workshop. An independent book editor, he teaches in the MFA creative writing program of the City College of New York.

Cynthia Hogue has published thirteen books, including nine collections of poetry, most recently *Revenance* (Red Hen Press, 2014), listed as one of the 2014 "Standout" books by the Academy of American Poets. With Sylvain Gallais, Hogue co-translated *Fortino Sámano* (The overflowing of the poem), from the French of poet Virginie Lalucq and philosopher Jean-Luc Nancy (Omnidawn 2012), which won the Harold Morton Landon Translation Award from the Academy of American Poets in 2013. She was a 2015 NEA Fellow in Translation, and holds the Maxine and Jonathan Marshall Chair in Modern and Contemporary Poetry at Arizona State University.

Doyali Farah Islam's poems have been published in *Kenyon Review Online, Grain*, and *Contemporary Verse 2*. She is the recipient of a 2015 Chalmers Arts Fellowship and past grants from Canada Council for the Arts, Ontario Arts Council, and Barbara Deming Memorial Fund. For two years, she curated Conspiracy of 3 Literary Reading Series out of North Bay, Ontario. Islam won Contemporary Verse 2's 2015 Young Buck Poetry Prize for writers under 35, as well as Arc Poetry Magazine's 2016 Poem of the Year. Her first poetry book was *Yusuf and the Lotus Flower* (BuschekBooks, 2011). Her current poetry manuscript is *heft and sing*. A Canadian poet, she lives in Toronto.

Genevieve Kaplan is the author of *In the ice house* (Red Hen Press, 2011), winner of the A Room of Her Own Foundation's poetry publication prize, and *settings for these scenes* (Convulsive Editions, 2013), a chapbook of continual erasures. She lives in southern California and edits the Toad Press International chapbook series, publishing contemporary translations of poetry and prose.

Vandana Khanna was born in New Delhi, India and received her MFA from Indiana University. Her first collection, *Train to Agra,* won the Crab Orchard Review First Book Prize (Southern Illinois University Press, 2001) and her second collection, *Afternoon Masala* (University of Arkansas Press, 2014), was the co-winner of the 2014 Miller Williams Poetry Prize. Her work has appeared in the *New England Review, The Missouri Review* and *Prairie Schooner* as well as the anthologies *Raising Lilly Ledbetter: Women Poets Occupy the Workspace, Asian American Poetry: The Next Generation* and *Indivisible: An Anthology of Contemporary South Asian American Poetry*.

Matthew Lippman is the author of 4 poetry collections—*The New Year of Yellow, Monkey Bars, Salami Jew,* and *American Chew*.

Beth Loffreda is a nonfiction writer and the author of *Losing Matt Shepard: Life and Politics in the Aftermath of Anti-Gay Murder* (Columbia, 2001) and, with Claudia Rankine and Max King Cap, *The Racial Imaginary* (Fence Books, 2015). She teaches creative writing and American Studies at the University of Wyoming.

Cecilia Llompart was born in Puerto Rico and raised in Florida. She received her BA from Florida State University, and her MFA from the University of Virginia. Her first collection, *The Wingless*, was published by Carnegie Mellon University Press in the spring of 2014. She is the recipient of two awards from the Academy of American Poets, and her work has been included or is forthcoming in many anthologies and journals. In 2015, she founded the literary nonprofit New Wanderers, a nomadic poetry collective that sponsors poets on long term travel projects. She currently divides her time between Paris and elsewhere.

Randall Mann is the author of three poetry collections: *Straight Razor* (Persea Books, 2013), *Breakfast with Thom Gunn* (University of Chicago Press, 2009), and *Complaint in the Garden* (Zoo Press, 2004). He lives in San Francisco.

Corey Marks is author of *Renunciation* (University of Illinois Press, 2000), a National Poetry Series selection, and *The Radio Tree* (New Issues Press, 2012), a Green Rose Prize winner. He's a University Distinguished Teaching Professor and directs creative writing at the University of North Texas.

Joyelle McSweeney is the author of 10 books of poetry, prose, essays, and plays, most recently the play *Dead Youth, or, The Leaks* (Litmus, 2014), winner of the inaugural Scalapino Prize for Women Performance Artists, and the poetics book *The Necropastoral: Poetry, Media, Occults* (University of Michigan Poets on Poetry Series, 2015). She coedits Action Books and teaches at Notre Dame.

Erika Meitner is the author of four books of poems, including *Copia* (BOA Editions, 2014); *Makeshift Instructions for Vigilant Girls* (Anhinga Press, 2011); and *Ideal Cities* (Harper Perennial, 2010), which was a 2009 National Poetry Series winner. She was recently the US-UK Fulbright Scholar in Creative Writing at the Seamus Heaney Centre for Poetry at Queen's University Belfast, and is currently an associate professor of English at Virginia Tech, where she directs the MFA program. You can find her at erikameitner.com.

Orlando Menes was born in Lima, Perú, to Cuban parents but has lived most of his life in the U.S. He is Professor of English at the University of Notre Dame, as well as the author of five poetry collections, most recently *Heresies* (University of New Mexico Press, 2015) and *Fetish*, winner of the 2012 Prairie Schooner Book Prize in Poetry. Menes has also published translations of poetry in Spanish, including *My Heart Flooded with Water: Selected Poems by Alfonsina Storni* (Latin American Literary Review Press, 2009). That same year he was awarded an NEA Fellowship.

Susan Laughter Meyers, of Givhans, SC, is the author of two full collections: *My Dear, Dear Stagger Grass* (Cider Press Review, 2013), winner of the *Cider Press Review* Editors Prize; and *Keep and Give Away* (University of South Carolina Press, 2006), winner of the SC Poetry Book Prize and a SIBA Book Award. Her chapbook *Lessons in Leaving* (1998) received the Persephone Press Book Award. Her work has also appeared in *The Southern Review, Prairie Schooner, Crazyhorse,* and other journals and anthologies. A long-time writing instructor, she has an MFA degree from Queens University of Charlotte.

Jennifer Militello is the author of *A Camouflage of Specimens and Garments* (Tupelo Press, 2016), *Body Thesaurus* (Tupelo Press, 2013), named one of the best books of 2013 by *Best American Poetry*, and *Flinch of Song*, winner of the Tupelo Press First Book Award. Her poems have appeared in *American Poetry Review, The Kenyon Review, The New Republic, The Paris Review, Ploughshares,* and *Best New Poets*. She teaches in the MFA program at New England College.

Tyler Mills is the author of *Tongue Lyre*, winner of the 2011 Crab Orchard Series in Poetry First Book Award (SIU Press, 2013). Her poems have appeared in *The*

New Yorker, Poetry, Boston Review, The Believer, Georgia Review, and *Blackbird,* and her creative nonfiction won the Copper Nickel Editor's Prize in Prose. She is editor-in-chief of *The Account: A Journal of Poetry, Prose, and Thought* and Assistant Professor of English at New Mexico Highlands University in Las Vegas, New Mexico.

Jacqueline Osherow's seventh collection *Ultimatum from Paradise* appeared in 2014. She's received grants from the NEA, Guggenheim, and Ingram Merrill Foundations and the Witter Bynner Prize from the American Academy and Institute of Arts and Letters. Her poems have appeared in many journals and anthologies, including *The New Yorker, The Paris Review, American Poetry Review, the Wadsworth Anthology of Poetry, The Longman Anthology of Poetry, Best American Poetry, The Norton Anthology of Jewish-American Literature, The Penguin Book of the Sonnet, Twentieth Century American Poetry* and *The Making of a Poem.* She's Distinguished Professor of English at the University of Utah.

Emilia Phillips is the author of two poetry collections from the University of Akron Press, *Signaletics* (2013) and *Groundspeed* (2016), and three chapbooks, most recently *Beneath the Ice Fish Like Souls Look Alike* (Bull City Press, 2015). Her poems and lyric essays appear in *Agni, Boston Review, Gulf Coast, Harvard Review, The Kenyon Review, New England Review, Ninth Letter, Ploughshares, Poem-a-Day* (Academy of American Poets), *Poetry,* and elsewhere. She is the Assistant Professor of Creative Writing at Centenary College of New Jersey.

Kevin Prufer's newest books are *Churches* (Four Way Books, 2014*), In a Beautiful Country* (Four Way Books, 2011), and *National Anthem* (Four Way Books, 2008). He has also edited numerous volumes, among them *New European Poets* (Graywolf, 2008; with Wayne Miller) and *Literary Publishing in the 21st Century* (Milkweed, 2016; with Wayne Miller and Travis Kurowski). Co-Curator of the Unsung Masters Series, he teaches in the Creative Writing Program at the University of Houston.

Claudia Rankine is the author of five books of poetry, including the bestseller *Citizen: An American Lyric,* (Graywolf, 2014) which won the National Book Critics Circle Award, the Forward Prize, the Los Angeles Times book award, the PEN Open Book Award, and the NAACP Image Award, and was a finalist for the National Book Award. She is a playwright, essayist, creator of video collaborations, and editor of many anthologies. A recipient of fellowships from the Academy of American Poetry, the National Endowments for the Arts, and the Lannan Foundation, she is a professor of Poetry at Yale University.

Joshua Robbins is the author of *Praise Nothing* (University of Arkansas Press, 2013). His recognitions include the New South Prize, the James Wright Poetry Award, and a Walter E. Dakin Fellowship in poetry from the Sewanee Writers' Conference. He teaches creative writing at the University of the Incarnate Word and lives in San Antonio.

Kathleen Rooney is a founding editor of Rose Metal Press, a publisher of literary work in hybrid genres, and a founding member of Poems While You Wait. Co-editor of *The Selected Writings of René Magritte*, forthcoming from Alma Books (UK) and University of Minnesota Press (U.S.) in 2016, she is also the author of seven books of poetry, nonfiction, and fiction, including, most recently, the novel *O, Democracy!* (Fifth Star Press, 2014) and the novel in poems *Robinson Alone* (Gold Wake Press, 2012). Her second novel, *Lillian Boxfish Takes a Walk*, will be published by St. Martin's Press in 2017.

Zach Savich is the author of five books of poetry, including *The Orchard Green and Every Color* (Omnidawn, 2016). His work has received the Iowa Poetry Prize, the Colorado Prize for Poetry, and the Cleveland State University Poetry Center's Open Award, among other honors. He teaches in the BFA Program for Creative Writing at the University of the Arts, in Philadelphia, and with Hilary Plum coedits Rescue Press's Open Prose Series.

Jeffrey Schultz is the author of the National Poetry Series Selection *What Ridiculous Things We Could Ask of Each Other* (University of Georgia Press, 2014). His poems have appeared in *Poetry*, *TriQuarterly*, and *Missouri Review*, and on *Poetry Daily*, *PBS NewHour's Art Beat*, and the Academy of American Poets' *Poem-a-Day*. He has received the "Discovery"/Boston Review prize and a Ruth Lily Fellowship from the Poetry Foundation. He teaches at Pepperdine University and lives in Los Angeles, California.

Martha Silano is the author of four books of poetry, including *The Little Office of the Immaculate Conception* (2011) and *Reckless Lovely* (2014), both from Saturnalia Books. She also coedited, with Kelli Russell Agodon, *The Daily Poet: Day-By-Day Prompts For Your Writing Practice* (Two Sylvias Press, 2013). Her poems have appeared in *Poetry*, *Paris Review*, *American Poetry Review*, *Orion*, and *The Best American Poetry 2009*, among others. Martha edits *Crab Creek Review* and teaches at Bellevue College.

Sean Singer is the author of *Discography* (Yale University Press, 2002), winner of the Yale Series of Younger Poets Prize, selected by W. S. Merwin, and the Norma Farber First Book Award from the Poetry Society of America; *Honey & Smoke* (Eyewear Publishing, 2015); and two chapbooks, *Passport* (Beard of Bees Press, 2007) and *Keep Right on Playing Through the Mirror Over the Water* (Beard of Bees Press, 2010). He is the recipient of a Fellowship from the National Endowment for the Arts. He has a PhD in American Studies from Rutgers-Newark. He drives a taxi for Uber in New York.

Marcela Sulak is the author of the poetry collections *Decency* (2015) and *Immigrant* (2010), both with Black Lawrence Press. She's coedited *Family Resemblance: An Anthology and Exploration of 8 Literary Hybrid Genres* (Rose Metal Press, 2015), and has translated four collections of poetry from the Hebrew, Czech, and French.

Her essays have appeared in *The Iowa Review*, and *The Los Angeles Review*, among others. Born and raised in Texas, Sulak directs the Shaindy Rudoff Graduate Program in Creative Writing at Bar-Ilan University in Israel.

Maureen Thorson is the author of two collections of poetry, *My Resignation* (Shearsman Books, 2014) and *Applies to Oranges* (Ugly Duckling Presse, 2011), as well as several chapbooks, most recently *The Woman, The Mirror, the Eye* (Bloof Books, 2015). She is at work on a book-length lyric essay about everything. Visit her at maureenthorson.com.

Afaa Weaver is the author of fourteen collections of poetry. *The Government of Nature* (University of Pittsburgh Press, 2013) won the 2014 Kingsley Tufts Award. *City of Eternal Spring* (University of Pittsburgh Press, 2014) won the 2015 Phillis Wheatley Book Award. Also a playwright, he completed his MA in Creative Writing (1987) at Brown University. His other awards include four Pushcarts and a Pew fellowship. As a translator, he works in contemporary Chinese poetry. Afaa is a native of Baltimore, Maryland.

Jillian Weise's latest collection, *The Book of Goodbyes* (BOA Editions, 2013) won the James Laughlin Award from the Academy of American Poets. Other books include *The Amputee's Guide to Sex* (Soft Skull Press, 2007) and *The Colony* (Counterpoint/Soft Skull Press, 2010). She teaches at Clemson University.

Valerie Wetlaufer is the author of the Lambda Award-winning collection *Mysterious Acts by My People* (Sibling Rivalry Press, 2014), and *Call Me by My Other Name* (Sibling Rivalry Press, 2016). She holds an MFA from Florida State University and a PhD from the University of Utah. Valerie lives in Cedar Rapids, Iowa.

Rachel Zucker is the author of nine books, most recently a double collection of poetry and prose, *The Pedestrians* (Wave Books, 2014), and a memoir, *MOTHERs* (Counterpath, 2014). She teaches poetry at NYU and lives in New York City.

Acknowledgments

Lisa Ampleman's "Paul and Fran" appeared in *Lake Effect*. Two sections of "Courtly Love (for Courtney Love)," "Bondage" and "Horseman," appeared in *Vinyl*.

Sandra Beasley's "The Sand Speaks" appears in *I Was the Jukebox* (W. W. Norton, 2011); "Let Me Count the Waves" appears in *Count the Waves* (W. W. Norton, 2015).

Susan Briante's "The Market as Composition" previously appeared in *Sentence*; it also appears in *The Market Wonders* (Ahsahta Press, 2016). Reprinted by permission of the author and Ahsahta Press. "June 14—The Dow Closes Down 10192" previously appeared in *Sous les paves*; it also appears in *The Market Wonders* (Ahsahta Press, 2016). Reprinted by permission of the author and Ahsahta Press.

Stephen Burt's "1978 Stephanie" first appeared in *Michigan Quarterly Review* and has also appeared in the chapbook *All-Season Stephanie* (Rain Taxi Editions, 2015). "A Nickel..." first appeared in *Virginia Quarterly Review*.

Jen Campbell's "Etymology" was first published in *The Rialto* poetry magazine.

Kara Candito's "Egypt Journal: The Poet's Condition" was first printed in *Blackbird* and is reproduced from *Taste of Cherry: Poems* by Kara Candito by permission of the University of Nebraska Press. Copyright 2009 by the Board of Regents of the University of Nebraska. "V's Dream on the Plane from Mexico City to Chicago" was originally printed in *The Indiana Review* and has also appeared in *Spectator* (University of Utah Press, 2014).

Bruce Cohen's "The Uncanny" first appeared in *Plume* and has also appeared in *Imminent Disappearances, Impossible Numbers & Panoramic X-Rays* (New Issues Poetry & Prose, 2016). "Follain Combs the Parking Lot for His Vehicle after the Movie" appeared in *Imminent Disappearances, Impossible Numbers & Panoramic X-Rays* (New Issues Poetry & Prose, 2016).

Erica Dawson's "Florida Officers Tied to KKK" first appeared in *North Dakota Quarterly*. "Ideation X" first appeared in *Virginia Quarterly Review* and has also appeared in *The Small Blades Hurt* (Measure Press, 2014).

Jehanne Dubrow's "Against War Movies" appeared in *Stateside*. Copyright© 2010 by Jehanne Dubrow. Published 2010 by TriQuarterly Books/Northwestern University Press. All rights reserved. "Fancy" appeared in *Red Army Red*. Copyright© 2012 by Jehanne Dubrow. Published 2012 by TriQuarterly Books/ Northwestern University Press. All rights reserved.

Rebecca Morgan Frank's "Crawfish Chorus," previously appeared in the anthology *The Gulf Stream: Poems of the Gulf Coast* (2013). "Juramentado," previously appeared in *Juried Reading, Book 15: The Poetry Center of Chicago* (Plastique Press, 2009).

Doyali Farah Islam's "the fishermen" and "trip to yarl's wood" both first appeared in *Contemporary Verse 2*.

Elisa Gabbert and Kathleen Rooney's, "Some Notes on the Weird" and "Some Notes on the Male Gaze" appeared in *The Kind of Beauty That Has Nowhere to Go* (Hyacinth Girl Press, 2013).

Hannah Gamble's "Hanging Out with Girls" first appeared in *American Poetry Review*. "Somewhere Golden" first appeared in *jubilat*.

Noah Eli Gordon, "For Expression" and "Against Erasure" appeared in *The Word Kingdom in the Word Kingdom* (Brooklyn Arts Press, 2014).

David Groff's "Clay's Flies" and "What's the Matter" both appeared in *Clay* (Trio House Press, 2013).

Cynthia Hogue's "in the meadow magenta" was featured on *Poem-a-Day;* "On Principle" was published in *Superstition Review*. Both were collected in *Revenance* (Red Hen Press, 2014).

Genevieve Kaplan's "The evening, the singing..." was previously published online at *Interrupture*, here: http://www.interrupture.com/archives/feb_2014/genevieve_kaplan/.

Vandana Khanna's "Echo" first appeared in *Rattle*; it also appeared in *Train to Agra* (SIU Press, 2001). "My Mother at JFK" first appeared in *Crab Orchard Review*; it also appeared in *Afternoon Masala*. Copyright 2014 by The University of Arkansas Press. Reproduced with the permission of the University of Arkansas Press, www.uapress.com.

Matthew Lippman's "Something About Ecology" first appeared in *Ploughshares*. "This Modern Life" first appeared in *Superstition Review*.

Beth Loffreda's "morning" was first published in *Boundary 2*. "The Racial Imaginary" appeared in *The Racial Imaginary: Writers on Race in the Life of the Mind* by Claudia Rankine and Beth Loffreda (Fence Books, 2015). Reprinted by permission of the authors and Fence Books.

Randall Mann's "?" and "Poem Beginning with a Line by John Ashbery" first appeared in *Complaint in the Garden* (Zoo Press, 2004). Reprinted by permission of the author.

Corey Marks' "The Black Bear at Closing" and "Three Bridges" first appeared in *The Radio Tree* (New Issues Poetry & Prose, 2012).

Joyelle McSweeney's verse play "The Contagious Knives" first appeared in *Percussion Grenade* (Fence, 2012). Reprinted by permission of the author and Fence Books.

Erika Meitner's "Swift Trucks" first appeared in *Pleiades*, and "Continuation" first appeared in *Shenandoah*.

Orlando Menes's "Doña Flora's Hothouse" first appeared in *The Indiana Review* and was subsequently collected in *Rumba Atop the Stones* (Peepal Tree Press, 2001). "Cenobites" first appeared in *Third Coast* and was subsequently collected in *Heresies* (University of New Mexico Press, 2015).

Susan Laughter Meyers' "The Tilt That Stumbles Me" was first published in *North Carolina Literary Review* and reprinted in *My Dear, Dear Stagger Grass* (Cider Press Review, 2013). "You Offer Apology" was first published in *Crazyhorse*.

Jennifer Militello's "A Dictionary of Preserving the Hydrangea's Bloom" first appeared in *The Kenyon Review*. "A Dictionary of Mechanics, Memory, and Skin in the Voice of Marian Parker" first appeared in *The Los Angeles Review* as winner of the Ruskin Art Club Poetry Prize. Both poems are included in *A Camouflage of Specimens and Garments*, published by Tupelo Press, copyright 2016 Jennifer Militello. Used with permission.

Tyler Mills, "Lesson" and "Cyclops," are from *Tongue Lyre* (Southern Illinois University Press, 2013). Previously, "Cyclops" appeared in *Memorious*.

Jacqueline Osherow's "Poem for Jenne" appeared in *Yale Review* and *Whitethorn* (LSU Press, 2011). "White on White" appeared in *Antioch Review* and *Ultimatum from Paradise* (LSU Press, 2014). Both poems were also featured on *Poetry Daily*.

Emilia Phillips' "Reading Ovid at the Plastic Surgeon's" first appeared in *Poetry* and "Aubade" first appeared in *The Freeman*. Both are collected in *Groundspeed* (University of Akron Press, 2016).

Kevin Prufer's "Bread & Cake" appeared on the Academy of American Poets' "Poem a Day" project. "How He Loved Them" appeared in *The Paris Review*. "Immigration" appeared in *Southern Review*.

Claudia Rankine, ["On the train the woman standing makes you understand there are no seats available."] from *Citizen: An American Lyric*. Copyright © 2014 by Claudia Rankine. Reprinted with the permission of The Permissions Company, Inc., on behalf of Graywolf Press, Minneapolis, Minnesota, www.

graywolfpress.org. 35 lines from *Citizen: An American Lyric* by Claudia Rankine (Penguin Books, 2015). Copyright © Claudia Rankine, 2014. Reproduced by permission of Penguin Books Ltd. "The Racial Imaginary" appeared in *The Racial Imaginary: Writers on Race in the Life of the Mind* by Claudia Rankine and Beth Loffreda (Fence Books, 2015). Reprinted by permission of the authors and Fence Books.

Joshua Robbins' "Exchange" was originally published in *Anti-*.

Martha Silano's "Ode to Frida Kahlo's Eyebrows" first appeared in the *North American Review*; it also appears in *Reckless Lovely* (Saturnalia Books, 2014). "Summons and Petition for Name Change" first appeared in *Drunken Boat*; it also appears in *Reckless Lovely* (Saturnalia Books, 2014).

Sean Singer's "Ancestors Who Came to New York" first appeared in *Moment*; it also appears in *Honey & Smoke* (Eyewear Publishing, 2015). "Embers of Smoldering Homes" first appeared in *The Rumpus*; it also appears in *Honey & Smoke* (Eyewear Publishing, 2015).

Marcela Sulak, "Avera" and "Union," from *Decency* (Black Lawrence Press, 2015).

Maureen Thorson, "Rocking the Pathetic Fallacy," from *My Resignation* (Shearsman Books, 2014).

Afaa Weaver, "City of Eternal Spring" from the book *City of Eternal Spring*, by Afaa Michael Weaver, © 2014. Reprinted by permission of the University of Pittsburgh Press. "To Those Who Would Awaken" from *The Government of Nature*, by Afaa Michael Weaver, © 2013. Reprinted by permission of the University of Pittsburgh Press.

Jillian Weise's "Biohack Manifesto" appeared in *POETRY* and was awarded the J. Howard and Barbara M. J. Wood Prize. "To Forget Mark Dicklip" appeared in *Crazyhorse*. "Semi Semi Dash" is from *The Book of Goodbyes*. Copyright © 2013 by Jillian Weise. Reprinted with the permission of The Permissions Company, Inc., on behalf of BOA Editions, Ltd., www.boaeditions.org.

Rachel Zucker, "real poem (appellation)" and "real poem (personal statement)" from *The Pedestrians*. Copyright 2014. Reprinted with permission of the author and Wave Books.

Card Catalogue

Fairytales, Plays, & Poems

Blogs, Constitutional Amendments, Supreme Court Cases, & Videos

Fauna

Proper Names

Proper Nouns

Who's Missing

We asked our contributors who was missing from this book, living or dead.

Kelli Russell Agodon
Jon Anderson
Russell Atkins
Daniel Borzutzky
Traci Brimhall
Jericho Brown
Heather Christle
CAConrad
Hart Crane
Geffrey Davis
Sor Juana Inés de la Cruz
Natalie Diaz
Emily Dickinson
Rita Dove
Camille Dungy
Russell Edson
Vievee Francis
Donald Hall
Ross Gay
Aracelis Girmay
Nicolas Guillen
Mark Halliday
June Jordan
Bhanu Kapil
Joy Ladin
Philip Larkin after several gins
Rickey Laurentiis
Sylvia Legris
Ada Limón
Tanya Lukin Linklater

Alain LeRoy Locke
René Magritte
Dawn Lundy Martin
Adrian Matejka
Jamaal May
Bernadette Mayer
Kerrin McCadden
Philip Metres
Wayne Miller
Pablo Neruda
Aimee Nezhukumatathil
Frank O'Hara
Matthew Olzmann
Steve Orlen
Yannis Ritsos
Patrick Rosal
Mary Ruefle
Jason Schneiderman
Peggy Shumaker
Carmen Giménez Smith
Gertrude Stein
Kim Trainor
Sarah Vap
Belle Waring
Marcus Wicker
William Wordsworth
C.D. Wright
John Yau
Jake Adam York
Matthew Zapruder